# PROFESSIONAL RECORDS AND INFORMATION MANAGEMENT

## Instructor's Manual

Jeffrey R. Stewart

Nancy M. Melesco

Glencoe
McGraw-Hill

New York, New York   Columbus, Ohio   Woodland Hills, California   Peoria, Illinois

## Glencoe/McGraw-Hill

*A Division of The* **McGraw·Hill** *Companies*

**Instructor's Manual and Key for** *Professional Records and Information Management,*
**Second Edition**

Send all inquiries to:
Glencoe/McGraw-Hill
21600 Oxnard Street, Suite 500
Woodland Hills, CA 91367-4947


Printed in the United States of America.


ISBN 0-07-822780-1


1 2 3 4 5 6 7 8 9 10    045    06 05 04 03 02 01

# CONTENTS

# INTRODUCTION

Records and information management (RIM) has become an accepted business profession because of the critical role played by its practitioners. RIM is also a vital academic domain that corresponds to accounting, law, finance, and marketing. Anyone preparing to enter the business or government sector today must have a basic knowledge of the management of records and information. In addition, many individuals who already work in business and government may wish to sharpen their RIM knowledge and skill. Thus, *Professional Records and Information Management*, Second Edition, has three major purposes:

- It serves as an introductory course for those who aspire to the profession of RIM.

- It provides the fundamental RIM information and vocabulary vital to all business students planning to pursue other specialties.

- It assists business and government employees in upgrading their skill and knowledge in the field of RIM.

## The Organization of *Professional Records and Information Management*, Second Edition

The twelve chapters of the textbook are grouped into three units:

- Unit 1, The Profession of Records and Information Management, contains three chapters dealing with introductory terminology and data about RIM, employment and professional associations in RIM, and legal and ethical concerns in RIM.

- Unit 2, Managing Nonelectronic Records, consists of four chapters that cover the paperwork overload confronting most businesses and organizations. Subject matter includes the receipt and creation of paper records, filing rules, filing systems, and the three Rs of records management—retrieval, retention, and recycling.

- Unit 3, Electronic Information Management, is comprised of five chapters that discuss current developments and technology in RIM. Coverage includes electronic files management, database systems, network-based file management, image technology, automated records systems, safety, security, and disaster recovery.

## Emphasis on Vocabulary

*ADA, BCS, carpal tunnel syndrome, CRM, disintegrator, electronic vaulting, ELF, freeze-drying technique, GUI, pulping, retinal eye pattern recognition, touch screen technology, voice-input computer,* and the *Web* are examples of the unique and emerging terminology that the records and information professional encounters daily. Only a few years ago, many of the above terms did not exist. These and more than 250 other specialized terms are introduced in *Professional Records and Information Management*, Second Edition. The text gives pronounced treatment to vocabulary in the following ways:

- Chapter key terms are listed in bold in the chapter opener.

- Key terms appear in the text in bold.

- Important terms appear in the text in italics.

- Marginal text notes highlight certain terminology.

- All new terms, both key and important, are listed at the end of each chapter.

- The end-of-chapter activities reinforce identifying key terms and important terms with their definitions.

- The glossary lists and defines more than 250 RIM terms used in the book.

- The chapter and comprehensive tests, which begin on page 29 of this manual, emphasize vocabulary.

## Emphasis on New Technology

Current technical developments in RIM are discussed and illustrated in the text. Examples include managing paper records with automated records systems, biometric access control devices, electronic file organization, ergonomics, the Internet, image technology, and integrated security systems.

## Legal and Ethical Matters

The text provides unique coverage of several of the legal terms, concepts, and requirements necessary to manage records in an information age. For example, the student learns to distinguish between civil and criminal litigation. Legal considerations, as they pertain to the retention and destruction of records, are discussed.

The records and information professional must recognize and practice good business ethics. The text focuses on the advantages (to the business, its owners, and its customers) of operating with high ethical standards in all matters, especially those dealing with RIM.

## Other Features of *Professional Records and Information Management*, Second Edition

The text has been designed for both group and individual instruction. Several features enhance its use in either setting:

- *Unit openers:* Each of the three units begins with a motivational, introductory profile of a real-life RIM professional.
- *Chapter purposes:* Every chapter opens with a list of the vital knowledge to be conveyed. Each purpose is stated in terms of student behavior or performance.
- *Marginal notes:* Marginal features summarize key concepts and present content questions.
- *Key terms:* Key terms from the chapter are listed in each chapter opener and are applied in end-of-chapter activities.
- *Documenting student learning:* Each chapter concludes with discussion and critical thinking questions on the chapter content. In most cases, answering these questions requires an understanding of ideas and concepts rather than mere technicalities.
- *Networking activities:* For each chapter, the last end-of-chapter activity requires the student to network with the real world by using the Internet to access information.
- *Unit professional activities:* At the end of each unit is a section called *Professional Activities*. It includes a series of student assignments under two headings: Implementing Concepts and Synthesizing Concepts. Under each of these headings is a group project to encourage cooperative learning and one individual project to foster personal development and introspection. The projects under the first heading require the student to apply the information presented in the unit, and the projects under the second heading require the student to use important critical thinking and higher-order reasoning skills.
- *Filing rule practice:* In Chapter 5, following the presentation of each filing rule, are exercises titled *Rule Practice*. These exercises provide

immediate reinforcement by requiring the student to apply the filing rule just presented. Additional filing rule practice exercises appear in Appendix A of the textbook. Answers to all Rule Practice exercises and Appendix A exercises appear in the back of the textbook.

- *Professional organizations and publications:* Appendices B and C provide the student with comprehensive lists of RIM professional organizations and periodicals related to the field.

### *Filing and Computer Database Projects,* Second Edition

A practice set titled *Filing and Computer Database Projects*, Second Edition, provides simulated experience in managing both paper and computer records. It includes an easy-to-use card file and a data disk. The practice set is designed to be finished in approximately thirty-two hours if all assignments and quizzes are completed. The practice set has a separate instructor's manual titled *Instructor's Manual and Key for Filing and Computer Database Projects*, Second Edition.

The practice set provides twelve hours of manual filing and records management practice as follows:

| ACTIVITY | HOURS |
|---|---|
| Alphabetic filing, individual names | 2 |
| Numeric filing | 1 |
| Alphabetic filing, business and government names | 2 |
| Geographic filing | 1 |
| Subject filing | 1 |
| Card filing quiz (in Instructor's Manual and Key) | 1 |
| Correspondence management (decision-making exercises) | 2 |
| Alphabetic and subject correspondence filing | 1 |
| Correspondence filing quiz (in Instructor's Manual and Key) | 1 |
| Total hours | 12 |

In addition, the practice set provides twenty-five hours of computer database projects. The computer database part of the practice set uses records from the same simulated businesses as the manual part. Thus students experience the conversion of manual records to electronic form. Students also gain an appreciation for the speed and efficiency of manipulating records by computer when those records have previously been dealt with manually. The approximately twenty-five hours consist of three computer database projects. Each project includes a performance quiz that requires the student to work with the database.

| ACTIVITY | HOURS |
|---|---|
| Managing a customer database | 5 |
| Managing an inventory database | 7 |
| Creating and managing an employee database | 13 |
| Total hours | 25 |

The data disk that comes with *Filing and Computer Database Projects*, Second Edition, includes the original records for the first two of the databases listed above—a total of 400 records that do not have to be input by the students. This database practice is more realistic than others because it has a relatively large number of records. Students will learn to appreciate the power and efficiency of a modern computer database. Data input practice is provided as part of each project when new customers, clients, products, and employees are added to the databases.

## Filing Rules Tutorial

The disk inside the back cover of the textbook contains a stand-alone filing rules tutorial of approximately eight to twelve hours of alphabetic filing utilizing the twelve ARMA-compatible filing rules. Its use reinforces Chapter 5 in *Professional Records and Information Management*, Second Edition.

## Gregg Quick Filing Practice

A popular alternative to *Filing and Computer Database Projects*, Second Edition, is *Gregg Quick Filing Practice*. This boxed set provides approximately twenty hours of manual filing practice, distributed as follows:

| ACTIVITY | HOURS |
|---|---|
| Alphabetic card filing and quiz | 9 |
| Alphabetic correspondence filing and quiz | 3 |
| Subject correspondence filing and quiz | 3 |
| Numeric card filing and quiz | 2 |
| Geographic card filing and quiz | 2 |
| Final test | 1 |
| Total hours | 20 |

## Scheduling Use of the Text and Practice Set

The textbook *Professional Records and Information Management*, Second Edition, and the practice set *Filing and Computer Database Projects*, Second Edition, are designed to be used together in a one-semester course. These materials can also be used in a one-quarter course by spending less time on the chapter and unit activities in the text and by omitting assignments 2, 3B, 5, 6B, and 7B in the practice set. The text and a practice set may also be used in units within courses by varying the emphasis given to textbook topics and by modifying practice set assignments.

# SUGGESTIONS FOR THE INSTRUCTOR AND KEYS TO END-OF-CHAPTER ACTIVITIES

## CHAPTER 1

## INTRODUCTION TO RECORDS AND INFORMATION MANAGEMENT

### Suggestions for the Instructor

1. Get the course off to a good start by getting to know your students and letting them get to know you. Have a class discussion in which you describe some of your experiences in dealing with matters related to records and information management. Give students an opportunity to share similar experiences with you and each other. Use the Unit 1 profile to introduce students to someone who works in the world of records and information management.

2. Relate to students another real-life example of someone who manages records for your school or other local organization. Have a summary of the person's duties prepared prior to your first session, and include this information in your class discussion.

3. Prepare a transparency from the master on page 110 of this manual. Use it to illustrate the steps in the life cycle of records.

### Key to Chapter 1 Terms

1. information system
2. non-record
3. contract
4. hard-copy
5. RIM or records and management
6. record

### Key to Chapter 1 Discussion Questions

1. Contracts, tax records, employment records, accounting records.

2. How businesses and other organizations plan, develop, and organize their information.

3. Creating, distributing, maintaining, protecting, controlling, storing, and eventually destroying the records created in an information system.

4. Yes, because if it costs more to create a record than the record is worth to a business, it probably should not be created at all. Costs include the expense of storage (physical space for paper or hard-copy documents; the medium for electronic storage) and retrieval as well as the cost of protecting the record.

5. Records being up to date, accurate, and relevant to the needed operation.

6. "Finding" or "retrieving a record." (*Instructor note:* Explain that if a stored record cannot be found, it is of no value to the organization.)

7. When records are no longer needed in the operations of the organization and when they are not required for legal reasons.

8. The steps in the life cycle of records.

# CHAPTER 2

# EMPLOYMENT IN RECORDS AND INFORMATION MANAGEMENT

## Suggestions for the Instructor

1. If possible, arrange to have a records and information management professional, perhaps a member of ARMA, speak to your class. Activities might include a discussion of employment opportunities, a description of the person's activities in a RIM professional organization, and questions from students.

2. Individuals who might provide valuable background information for this chapter include the school librarian, a medical office employee, a legal office employee, and a financial manager in your school or other organization.

3. Newspaper classified employment advertisements are an excellent source of background information for this chapter. National business newspapers such as the *Wall Street Journal* often contain want ads for higher-level positions such as chief information officer (CIO).

## Key to Chapter 2 Discussion Questions

1. Large organizations, corporations, museums, libraries, and records storage centers.

2. Designing records systems, updating records, and designing controls to ensure financial records integrity.

3. Deeds, wills, birth certificates, marriage records, and tax records. (*Instructor note:* Ask students if they can think of others that are not listed in the text. Examples include police records, divorce records, land transfer records, and property tax assessments.)

4. Business, medical technology, medical records, nursing, insurance, and health care services.

5. Filming of records, disaster recovery, and records destruction.

6. Because business and government records continue to become more numerous while legal record keeping requirements become more complex.

7. Association of Records Managers and Administrators, Inc. (ARMA International). Benefits to members include continuing education, technical publications, local seminars, certification studies, *The Information Management Journal*, and thirty-four industry specific groups for networking.

8. The Institute of Certified Records Managers (ICRM).

9. Professional organizations provide advantages such as professional identity, unity, networking opportunities, leadership opportunities, the promotion of education and training, and access to professional information.

# CHAPTER 3

# LEGAL AND ETHICAL MATTERS IN RECORDS AND INFORMATION MANAGEMENT

## Suggestions for the Instructor

1. Have students bring to class newspaper stories about court cases. As part of a class discussion, ask students to identify which cases involve criminal law and which involve civil law.

2. Be sure that students understand the difference between the private sector and the public sector. Discuss types of operations that might be either, depending on whether they are owned by a government (public) agency or by private owners or shareholders. Examples include a private tour bus company versus a public bus

authority, the government-operated Federal Reserve System versus a commercial bank, and a privately owned theme park versus a state or national park.

3. Obtain information from a placement officer or guidance counselor about the rights of a job applicant when supplying information to a prospective employer. Discuss with students the type of information they are not required to reveal about themselves when they apply for a job.

4. Initiate a class discussion about ethical issues in business, especially as they relate to RIM. The purpose of the discussion might be to make students fully aware of the advantages of ethical business behavior, especially over time.

9. Ensure that documents are destroyed only as part of a planned, approved program; be aware of any litigation against your company; refrain from destroying relevant records during litigation; and become familiar with your state's rules on admissibility into evidence.

10. Because the likely result of ethical business management includes desirable results, such as customer loyalty, high employee productivity, and greater sales; likely results of unethical practices are the opposite.

11. Maintaining confidentiality of records, ensuring high-quality service in the management of information, and reporting honestly to management and regulatory agencies on RIM activities. (*Instructor note:* Encourage students to name other examples of ethical policies.)

## Key to Chapter 3
## Discussion Questions

1. The difference has to do with the parties in the dispute. Criminal law involves legal action by the government against a violator of law or regulation; civil law involves a legal disagreement between one person or company and another.

2. How private sector records are kept, how public sector records are kept, and the rights and responsibilities of citizens related to records and information.

3. The business records themselves.

4. To streamline how federal government information is kept by reducing the number and volume of paper records.

5. The right of access to (1) information about the operation of federal government agencies and (2) information that is on file about themselves.

6. The Privacy Act of 1974.

7. Duplicate copyrighted items only with the permission of the owner, refrain from duplicating official government items such as paper money, and refrain from illegally duplicating copyrighted computer software. (Any two constitute a correct answer.)

8. Because litigation has become more common in recent years.

# CHAPTER 4

# RECEIPT AND CREATION OF HARD COPY RECORDS

## Suggestions for the Instructor

1. An important focus of Chapter 4 is to instill in students a positive attitude toward paperwork reduction. Many business operations are hampered because of excessive reports and memos, junk mail, redundant copies, and other useless information on paper. The instructor might collect incoming mail for one week and take it to class one day. Allow students to comment on which items are records to be filed, which are to be kept temporarily until acted on, and which might reasonably be discarded or deposited for recycling immediately. In a class discussion, try to get students to think about some of the costs of excessive paperwork: lost productivity due to paper shuffling, equipment and facility cost for paper storage, difficulty in locating records of importance, disposal costs, and damage to the environment.

2. If your school has a copy center or duplicating facility, obtain information (or have students do so) about how copy costs are controlled, how machine access is controlled, how unauthorized copying is prevented, how the production of excessive numbers of copies is discouraged, and whether or not unusable copies are deposited for recycling. Share this information with your students, or have them report their findings to the class.

3. Obtain a business form from your school or other organization. Have small groups of students critique the form and develop a new design. Permit students to vote on the winning forms design. Post all revised forms on a bulletin board.

4. Obtain form-filling software and appoint a group of students to (1) install and learn the software and (2) demonstrate how it can be used to fill out forms at a computer.

## Key to Chapter 4 Discussion Questions

1. Technological developments such as copying machines, plain-paper fax machines, laser and inkjet printers, high-speed mainframe computer printers, and low-cost offset printing equipment have all made it easier and more tempting to produce paperwork. Also, many local, state, and federal government regulations require more record keeping each year.

2. Any kind of mail that is on paper.

3. Prioritize; separate first-class mail from the rest.

4. If the paperwork costs more to keep than it is worth to the organization, it should be discarded.

5. No; an alternative would be to keep a copy on computer disk.

6. Work schedules, pay notices to employees, internal company newsletters, company policies and procedures, and requests for information. (Any three comprise a correct answer.)

7. Computer records and e-mail.

8. Print them single-spaced and on both sides of the paper.

9. On the back.

10. Form-filling software saves time by aligning copy to be filled in with the blank spaces on the form.

# CHAPTER 5

# INDEXING AND ALPHABETIZING PROCEDURES

## Suggestions for the Instructor

1. Have students index and alphabetize their own names and the names of local businesses and organizations.

2. Point out differences in the ARMA compatible rules and how names are alphabetized in the local telephone directory.

3. Use the filing rules tutorial disk in the back cover of the text for independent study of the filing rules.

4. Use the available practice set, *Filing and Computer Database Projects*, Second Edition. Assignments 1, 2, 4, and 5 provide practice on the contents of this chapter.

5. For supplementary practice, have students complete the additional indexing and alphabetizing workouts in Appendix A of the textbook.

## Key to Chapter 5 Terms

1. indexing
2. alphabetizing
3. uppercase
4. unit
5. alphabetic filing
6. lowercase

## Key to Chapter 5
## Discussion Questions

1. Each part of a name that is considered separately when that name is indexed.
2. Determining the order and format of the units in a name when alphabetizing.
3. Arranging names in alphabetic order.
4. Refers to whether letters of the alphabet are written in small (lowercase) letters (for example, a) or in capital (uppercase) letters (for example, A).

**Instructor note:** The keys to the Chapter 5 rule practice and the Appendix A additional indexing and alphabetizing practice appear in the back of the student textbook.

# CHAPTER 6

# SYSTEMS FOR ORGANIZING PAPER RECORDS

## Suggestions for the Instructor

1. Provide each student with a standard file folder and a file folder label. Allow students to attach file labels, crease expansion scores, and place papers correctly into the folders.
2. Demonstrate how folders are stored in file cabinets, and permit students to store and retrieve files.
3. Determine (or have students determine) how vital records at your school or other organization are protected from fire or other disaster. Discuss the results of the inquiry in class.
4. Determine (or have students determine) specific policies at your school or other organization related to compliance with the Americans with Disabilities Act.
5. Use the available practice set, *Filing and Computer Database Projects*, Second Edition.

Assignments 1 through 12 provide practice and evaluation related to the contents of Chapters 4 through 6.

## Key to Chapter 6
## Discussion Questions

1. To support file folders and to label major sections of the file.
2. They are more expensive to purchase and repair than manually operated equipment.
3. Design, color, acoustical treatment, security, safety, accessibility, and the relationship of the equipment to other office furnishings and accessories.
4. The Americans with Disabilities Act (ADA).
5. They are more costly to use than standard-size equipment and paper.
6. Additional floor space, extra labor for handling records, and extra time for finding and retrieving paper records.
7. Time and labor to convert paper to another format and the cost of special equipment needed to operate a paperless system.
8. Chronologically, or by date.
9. With the heading to the left and the front facing the user.
10. The record is examined to determine the name under which it is to be filed, the name is indexed according to the filing rules, and the indexed name is noted on the record.
11. Those which refer to products, processes, formulas, and other matters without containing the name of a person or organization.
12. Dictionary subject files have alphabetized captions and no subheadings; encyclopedic subject files have both main headings and subheadings.
13. A sales business with geographic sales areas.
14. They are (1) easier to expand, (2) more accurate for large files, (3) less likely to have duplicate captions, and (4) more secure. (Any three constitute a correct answer.)
15. You must know the number of a form to find it in the files, or an alphabetic index must be established.

# CHAPTER 7

## RETRIEVAL, RETENTION, AND RECYCLING

### Suggestions for the Instructor

1. When discussing the function of records retrieval, contrast the five major components (access, documentation, delivery, follow-up, and recovery) in a small business office with those in a large office.

2. Determine (or have students determine) how long selected records are kept and why in a business or organization office. Discuss findings in class.

3. Have students investigate which organizations and businesses in the community use recycled paper or have a recycling program. Have them report on the experiences of those who have adopted recycling policies and programs. If the local government has a recycling program, invite the director or other employee to speak to your class about advantages and problems associated with such a program.

### Key to Chapter 7 Discussion Questions

1. Electronic access from a desk terminal connected to a network.

2. The location from which the record was removed, the name of the record, the person who borrowed it, the date on which it was borrowed, and the date on which it is to be returned.

3. To ensure the timely return of borrowed records.

4. The original record is always available for others to use and the next two components of retrieval, follow-up and recovery, can be disregarded.

5. The user is reminded, if necessary, that borrowed records are due.

6. They should be inspected for completeness and possible damage.

7. Records retention.

8. They are numerous, intricate, and can differ from one locality and state to another.

9. Cost, security, and environmental protection.

10. They can be read by others and they may not be recycled.

11. They all provide security by making records unreadable.

12. Trees, water, and landfill space.

# CHAPTER 8

## MANAGING ELECTRONIC FILES

### Suggestions for the Instructor

1. Because Chapter 8 is vocabulary intensive, you can divide the class into two groups and have a competitive quiz program on the terms listed at the end of the chapter. Have students develop the quiz program format and rules. The instructor may act as moderator.

2. As a test of student knowledge of the many new terms in this chapter, ask the class to configure a hypothetical computer. Students might log onto the Web site of an electronic retailer or visit a local electronics store to obtain information about a desktop computer. When they have gathered the information, have them review their choices in class and justify their decisions.

3. Have students devise a document tracking number system for files sent to recipients outside the company. The rules should allow others in the class to create a code based on the author, recipient, date, and/or type of document.

4. Store one or more Microsoft Word documents on a network file server or on individual lab computers. Have students use the Advanced Find function of MS Word to locate the document using information you provide, such as the date the document was created, the manager, and keywords (but not the file name).

## Key to Chapter 8
## Discussion Questions

1. The physical components of the computer; types include the CPU; input devices such as the keyboard, a mouse, a microphone, a video camera, and a document scanner; output devices such as the monitor, the printer, speakers, storage devices.

2. Electronic containers that can contain files and/or other folders or directories.

3. An example might be

   h:\
   ├─homeowners
   ├─automobile
     ├─Kopecky S.
       ├─police_report.021501.doc

4. Descriptive information about files that can be recorded; you can "show properties" to get more information about a file that you think is the one you need to retrieve or you can use the Advanced Search option to search for a document using key words, phrases, or date ranges.

5. a. Principle of Identification: briefly describe the contents of a file for ease of location. Examples might be *Series1PriceList.xls, ProgrammerBJobQualifications.doc*.

   b. Principle of Brevity: keep the file name a reasonable length so it can be viewed in a browser window. Examples might be *MktTest Denver.doc, StegallJStockPortfolio.xls*.

   c. Principle of Documentation: used to distinguish documents that might occur many times by including in the file name such things as the date, author, chronological sequence, type, importance, retention period, destruction date, version, security level, and subject. Examples might be *FruendRichard.letter.20010723.doc, NorfleetCoOrderNMM 010625*.

6. Answers will vary. Examples might include:

   a. SpearsRecommend

   b. ComstockQuoteRqst

   c. PrelimLateFees

   d. E-Toys_FallPresentation

7. (1) Start the application used to create the document and open the document from within the application; (2) use the operating system tools, such as a file browser, to locate and open the document.

8. (1) Send it as an attachment to an e-mail message, (2) send a pointer to the document, or (3) give or send a hard copy of the document to the coworker.

9. Electronic storage devices can become corrupt or damaged, and it is necessary to protect against the accidental destruction of documents; backups should be done regularly; a full backup should be done periodically, and incremental backups can be done more often.

# CHAPTER 9

# USING ELECTRONIC DATABASES

## Suggestions for the Instructor

1. Demonstrate, or have students demonstrate, an existing database. Show (or have students show) how the information in the tables relates to what appears in the forms and reports.

2. Have students design a database for the school.

3. Use the available practice set, *Filing and Computer Database Projects*, Second Edition. Projects Three and Four provide practice and evaluation on the use of an existing database. Project Five requires students to create a database from scratch.

4. Have each student find and analyze a Web-based database (most news sites, portals, and e-stores use databases). Have students hypothesize table organization and fields based on how the site works. Then have the students pose a problem and possible solution (a query) that the site cannot do currently.

## Key to Chapter 9 Terms

2. a. database management system

   b. memo

   c. relational database

d. query

e. table

f. field

g. key

h. number

i. date

j. link

# Key to Chapter 9
# Discussion Questions

1. One category of storage that cannot be broken down any further; examples include a part number, part description, quantity on hand, quantity on order, and bin number (location).

2. All the fields related to one customer, employee, vendor, client, person, company, organization, product, case, or item.

3. A group of related records.

4. Because zip codes can be in either 5 digit or 9 digit form; the 9 digit codes need to be sorted based on the first 5 digits first, then the last 4, and storing the zip code as a string will accomplish this.

5. A form gives people the ability to easily input, modify, or read information stored in tables, usually one record at a time.

6. A date field.

7. Tables, forms, reports and queries are the primary parts of a modern DBMS.

8. A query.


# CHAPTER 10

# NETWORK-BASED RECORDS MANAGEMENT

## Suggestions for the Instructor

1. Have some students create a shared folder with permissions for other students to access (or give the share a password). Have students attempt to retrieve a document from another computer using the created share.

2. Have students search the Internet for information about a particular records management topic or product. For example, you might have them research paper document storage systems.

3. If your lab computers are on a Windows domain of if they are running Microsoft Windows NT or Windows 2000, have students give read-only permission to a group or individual for a file or folder. Then have students change the rights to *no access* on a different file or folder. Discuss the results.

**Instructor note:** This project will be easier if it is done on a shared folder like those created in Suggestion 1.


# Key to Chapter 10
# Discussion Questions

1. A client computer is the one that requests information; the server is the computer that supplies the information to the client who requested it.

2. A peer computer both requests and gives information.

3. Protocol is the set of rules for communication between computers. It allows computers to be able to establish communication and to exchange information.

4. A Local Area Network that connects the computers within a company or organization.

5. http://www.fultonmotors.com

6. Answers should include:

   a. Ensure that there is a *definitive* version of a document.

   b. Allow access control to electronic records by using file permissions.

   c. Track who accesses the electronic records by keeping a log on the server.

   d. Protect records by regularly backing up the server.

7. A metasearch requests a Web search by several search engines and returns all their results,

whereas a regular search uses a single search engine.

8. Use a search engine and enter the words *records management*.

# CHAPTER 11

## IMAGE TECHNOLOGY AND AUTOMATED SYSTEMS

## Suggestions for the Instructor

1. Arrange for the class to visit a media facility or library equipped with micrographic and optical disk technology.

2. Have students collect samples of bar codes from various sources. If they have specific information, permit them to describe to the class the use of each bar code.

3. Demonstrate, or have students demonstrate, the use of computer software used to keep track of paper records and other information.

4. Obtain from ARMA (see Appendix B of the textbook for the address) their current *Software Directory for Automated Records Management Systems*. As a student project, have a group of students study the directory and report to the class on the number, types, cost, and features of the software listed.

5. Demonstrate, or have students demonstrate, the use of a wildcard in locating information.

## Key to Chapter 11 Discussion Questions

1. The conversion of paper records to photographic or electronic form and administering them in the new form.

2. Input, or capture; indexing; storing; and retrieving.

3. Real images are exact representations of paper records, whereas data images consist of certain information captured from a paper record.

4. Microfilm is in rolls; microfiche consists of flat sheets.

5. An image scanner converts paper records to electronic images; a microfilmer converts paper records to miniature filmed images.

6. To look at documents that have been microfilmed.

7. It has the potential for even greater savings of time, money, and space.

8. Compact disk-recordable (CD-R), compact disk-rewritable (CD-RW), digital video disk (DVD), hard disk, and redundant array of inexpensive disks (RAID).

9. BCS, MICR, OCR, ICR, and OMR.

10. Bar coding technology.

11. Bar code scanner and bar code sorter.

12. Reports are generated and sent directly to disk rather than being printed and later scanned.

13. Because they are not accessible quickly by computer.

14. Conventional systems usually do not require the purchase of new hardware; imaging or full-text systems do. Conventional systems do not allow viewing of the contents of records; imaging or full-text systems do.

15. Law and medicine.

16. System functions, cost, and architecture.

17. Automatic calculation of retention periods for all active and inactive records, identification of vital records, and notification and confirmation of records due for destruction.

18. Increased operational efficiency and better service for those who have access to and use records.

19. Global modifications.

20. The initial outlay as well as the long-term maintenance, support, and training costs of the system.

21. To determine whether or not the system will work with existing computing gear, and to determine the possibility of purchasing or leasing new hardware and perhaps employing experts who will be able to work with complex systems.

# CHAPTER 12

# SAFETY, SECURITY, AND DISASTER RECOVERY

## Suggestions for the Instructor

1. Demonstrate the safe use of file equipment. Emphasize keeping file drawers closed, avoiding top-heavy loads, and exercising caution in the use of electrical equipment.

2. Have students research and report on recent fires and other disasters in businesses. Their class reports might include how records were recovered, possible losses, and insurance problems related to the loss of records.

3. Determine (or have students determine) how the student records of your school are kept secure. If the records are electronic, determine how passwords are assigned and what levels of passwords exist. If records are paper, determine how they are protected from loss in the event of a disaster. Discuss findings in class.

## Key to Chapter 12 Discussion Questions

1. Develop a written, comprehensive safety plan.

2. It might tip over, perhaps onto the file worker.

3. Check to see that the power switch is in the off position.

4. Consider the use of an ergonomic keyboard, schedule keying activities at less frequent intervals, and use other input devices such as scanners and voice-input computers.

5. Improper access, accidental loss, theft, damage, and unwanted destruction.

6. Unique physical characteristics of the employee such as fingerprint, voice, retinal or iris eye pattern, handprint and facial characteristics, and signature recognition.

7. Carefully weigh its potential benefits against its cost.

8. Failure to save a file, accidentally erasing a disk or other electronic medium, loss of floppy disks because they have been misplaced or stolen, crashing of a computer hard disk, computer viruses, and damage to hardware and software from natural and human disasters. (Any three constitute a correct response.)

9. To protect the data in a computer or computer network by controlling user access.

10. Alter and destroy data.

11. The increased volume of records, the use of electronic databases that can be wiped out quickly, and the increased importance of records to the survival of the organization.

12. (1) Being ready for natural disasters and having backup records in a location not likely to be affected by the disaster, and (2) trying to prevent human disasters and minimizing loss if they do occur.

13. Disaster recovery.

14. Freeze-drying and air-drying.

# SUGGESTIONS FOR THE INSTRUCTOR FOR UNIT-ENDING PROFESSIONAL ACTIVITIES

## UNIT 1

## THE PROFESSION OF RECORDS AND INFORMATION MANAGEMENT

### Implementing Unit 1 Concepts

#### Group Activity and Individual Inquiry

If one of the professional associations listed in Appendix B has a chapter in your area, get in touch with an officer to request interviews for your students for the group activity and for the individual inquiry.

### Synthesizing Unit 1 Concepts

#### Group Activity

Following is a sample report addressing this project:

*Professional RIM Consultants* is a specialized company that assists legal and medical firms in the private sector in maintaining accurate records that can be located easily and quickly when needed. Company consultants are aware of the large volumes of records these professions must keep. They are also aware of technical and legal matters associated with the legal and health professions. The company employs experienced and knowledgeable consultants who specialize in records and information management. All the consultants are required to have experience working in a legal or medical environment.

*Professional RIM Consultants* is equipped with state-of-the-art technological equipment and soft-ware. This equipment permits the staff to perform records surveys efficiently and accurately. After each survey, consultants can make sound recommendations for improving the client's records system.

*Professional RIM Consultants* employs professionals, all of whom are members of ARMA International. The consultants and other employees adhere to a mission statement that is similar to ARMA's. The mission is to (1) advance the practice of records and information management as a discipline and a profession; (2) organize and promote programs of research, education, training, and communication within the profession; (3) enhance the professionalism of the consultants; (4) promote cooperative endeavors with related professional groups; (5) set consulting fees to ensure reasonable profit as well as client trust and loyalty; (6) be straightforward in advertising so that clients understand the conditions of service they will receive; and (7) maintain and ensure a strict, confidential relationship with all clients.

The employees at *Professional RIM Consultants* are considered the most valuable asset of the organization. The company is committed to treating every employee with respect and fairness. This attitude extends to matters related to pay and benefits. Owners and managers believe in instilling, by example, positive attitudes and ethical values in all employees. In doing so, owners and managers state that they can strengthen both the company and its employees. They believe in the importance of enhancing employees' overall enjoyment and fulfillment in the work they do for the company.

#### Individual Inquiry

The following sample response might help the instructor guide students as they begin this individual inquiry project:

As a RIM employee, I must ensure that documents are destroyed only as part of a planned, approved program. It is important that I refrain from destroying any records because I am also aware of a litigation that is pending against my company about the product in question. I might explain to my employer that these documents may be relevant to the case and that it is against the law to destroy any documents purposely while a case is still pending. Finally, as a custodian of records, I should become familiar with the rules in my state about the admissibility into evidence of business documents and records. I should be aware that there are court rules governing the admissibility into evidence of an original document or a photocopy, microfilm copy, or computer software copy of that document.

# UNIT 2

## MANAGING NONELECTRONIC RECORDS

## Implementing Unit 2 Concepts

### Group Activity

Schedule each group to present the outcomes of this group activity. If possible, provide time for interaction and discussion with members of the other groups.

### Individual Inquiry

This inquiry can also be completed cooperatively by small groups of students (two or three to a group).

## Synthesizing Unit 2 Concepts

### Group Activity

Depending on the state where students live, perhaps half of all health-related paperwork pertains to insurance. A suggested method for reducing health insurance paperwork is to send patient information, status, and fees data to the insurance organization via properly secured e-mail. This method will eliminate multiple copies of insurance claim forms.

A patient database system can also reduce the health care establishment's internal paperwork if the physicians and nurses are allowed access to the database. During a patient's visit, the physician could enter the symptoms, prognosis, and remedy recommendations directly into that patient's file in the database instead of writing the same information on paper and having someone else key it in later.

### Individual Inquiry

A sample answer for topic 1:

It is likely that someone whose personality is Type A (a person who is always busy doing many tasks at one time) will be better organized than a Type B individual (a person who does one task at a time). The Type A person will tend to be highly organized with his or her records so a high performance rate can be maintained. Conversely, the Type B person will tend to be more nonchalant and therefore not make the extra effort to establish and maintain a highly organized filing system.

A sample answer for topic 4:

This business should devise a method to reduce the number of copies made by employees. Reduction of copies can be done by (1) reducing memorandum distribution and copy lists, (2) posting bulletins via e-mail instead of distributing paper bulletin copies to each employee, and (3) assigning account numbers to each employee so everyone will have to log on and log off when using a copy machine.

# UNIT 3

## ELECTRONIC INFORMATION MANAGEMENT

## Implementing Unit 3 Concepts

### Group Activity

Designs will vary widely by student group and by institution. This activity is recommended as a follow-up for Project 5 in the *Filing and Computer Database Projects*, Second Edition, practice set.

### Individual Inquiry

This inquiry might also be completed by small groups of students.

# Synthesizing Unit 3 Concepts

## Group Activity

An alternative to this activity is to have a local government official speak to the class about disaster recovery.

## Individual Inquiry

Common themes that might appear in students' recommendations are listed below:

1. The organization should upgrade its electronic database hardware and software.

2. The organization should retrain the users of the upgraded system.

3. As part of the organization's disaster preparedness plan, managers should devise several effective backup methods rather than only one.

4. The organization should consistently and routinely perform quality assurance checks on the information in the databases.

5. The organization should install more effective security measures to prevent natural and human disasters.

Possible reaction from management to students' recommendations:

After management hears the students' recommendations, managers might say that recommendations are not cost-effective and therefore are not acceptable. In some cases where managers dismissed the students' recommendations, the experience can affect the students' self-esteem and attitude toward records and information management. The instructor should hold an open discussion about how the students feel after such an experience.

# KEYS TO CHAPTER TESTS, FORM A

## OBJECTIVE TESTS

### Chapter 1, Form A

| | |
|---|---|
| 1. c | 11. T |
| 2. a | 12. F |
| 3. d | 13. T |
| 4. b | 14. F |
| 5. b | 15. T |
| 6. d | 16. F |
| 7. c | 17. F |
| 8. a | 18. T |
| 9. d | 19. F |
| 10. a | 20. F |

### Chapter 2, Form A

| | |
|---|---|
| 1. h | 14. T |
| 2. c | 15. T |
| 3. n | 16. T |
| 4. b | 17. T |
| 5. m | 18. F |
| 6. k | 19. F |
| 7. d | 20. T |
| 8. a | 21. T |
| 9. i | 22. F |
| 10. f | 23. T |
| 11. e | 24. F |
| 12. j | 25. T |
| 13. F | |

### Chapter 3, Form A

| | |
|---|---|
| 1. d | 11. T |
| 2. c | 12. F |
| 3. b | 13. F |
| 4. f | 14. T |
| 5. e | 15. T |
| 6. b | 16. F |
| 7. d | 17. T |
| 8. d | 18. T |
| 9. a | 19. F |
| 10. c | 20. T |

### Chapter 4, Form A

| | |
|---|---|
| 1. g | 14. b |
| 2. c | 15. c |
| 3. h | 16. F |
| 4. l | 17. F |
| 5. a | 18. T |
| 6. k | 19. T |
| 7. i | 20. F |
| 8. d | 21. T |
| 9. f | 22. F |
| 10. e | 23. T |
| 11. a | 24. F |
| 12. c | 25. T |
| 13. d | |

### Chapter 5, Form A

| | |
|---|---|
| 1. f | 21. Wise |
| 2. a | 22. United |
| 3. c | 23. Canada |
| 4. e | 24. R |
| 5. d | 25. Roy |
| 6. Slate | 26. cab |
| 7. MacDonald | 27. cab |
| 8. EllisKandies | 28. cab |
| 9. Roasty | 29. bac |
| 10. deHinesto | 30. bca |
| 11. OReilly | 31. acb |
| 12. Claddock | 32. cab |
| 13. Dr | 33. abc |
| 14. Liz | 34. acb |
| 15. Larrys | 35. acb |
| 16. 4 | 36. abc |
| 17. 9 | 37. cab |
| 18. SixtyForty | 38. bac |
| 19. 7 | 39. acb |
| 20. 98cent | 40. cba |

## Chapter 6, Form A

1. d
2. i
3. m
4. a
5. q
6. n
7. b
8. r
9. k
10. f
11. v
12. j
13. o
14. h
15. p
16. e
17. g
18. s
19. c
20. l
21. b
22. a
23. d
24. b
25. c
26. F
27. F
28. T
29. T
30. F
31. T
32. F
33. F
34. T
35. F

## Chapter 7, Form A

1. b
2. e
3. i
4. l
5. f
6. k
7. a
8. g
9. j
10. d
11. T
12. T
13. T
14. F
15. F
16. T
17. T
18. F
19. T
20. T

## Chapter 8, Form A

1. d
2. c
3. c
4. a
5. d
6. c
7. c
8. b
9. d
10. b
11. c
12. d
13. h
14. l
15. e
16. j
17. g
18. a
19. k
20. i
21. F
22. T
23. T
24. T
25. F
26. T
27. T
28. T
29. F
30. F
31. filetype
32. Find
33. shortcuts
34. floppy
35. application or program
36. output devices
37. criteria or requirements
38. digital signature
39. number
40. file name or full file name

## Chapter 9, Form A

1. n
2. c
3. g
4. f
5. b
6. k
7. i
8. m
9. d
10. h
11. c
12. d
13. b
14. c
15. d
16. b
17. a
18. c
19. c
20. c
21. T
22. F
23. T
24. F
25. T
26. T
27. F
28. F
29. T
30. F
31. a
32. c
33. c
34. a
35. c
36. e
37. h
38. f
39. h
40. f
41. b or g
42. c
43. d
44. h
45. b

## Chapter 10, Form A

1. b
2. d
3. c
4. d
5. c
6. c
7. d
8. c
9. c
10. b
11. h
12. c
13. e
14. b
15. g
16. i
17. d
18. a
19. j
20. k
21. F
22. T
23. T
24. F
25. T
26. F
27. T
28. T
29. F
30. F
31. gov
32. read
33. top/sales/kentucky/oct.html
34. mapped drive
35. protocols
36. network media or media
37. one of:
    console emulation, Telnet, or
    Remote Access Service (RAS)
38. domain name
39. client
40. method or protocol

## Chapter 11, Form A

1. j
2. p
3. n
4. b
5. e
6. g
7. d
8. a
9. l
10. c
11. h
12. f
13. o
14. i
15. k
16. T
17. F
18. T
19. T
20. F
21. F
22. F
23. T
24. F
25. T
26. T
27. T
28. F
29. T
30. F
31. p
32. d
33. i
34. b
35. c
36. g
37. a
38. k
39. f
40. j
41. n
42. l
43. r
44. o
45. q
46. a
47. c
48. b
49. d
50. d

## Chapter 12, Form A

1. e
2. n
3. j
4. l
5. c
6. k
7. b
8. m
9. h
10. d
11. T
12. F
13. T
14. F
15. F
16. F
17. T
18. F
19. T
20. T
21. d
22. a
23. c
24. b
25. b
26. c
27. f
28. l
29. b
30. i
31. e
32. g
33. j
34. h
35. a

# KEYS TO CHAPTER TESTS, FORM B

## OBJECTIVE TESTS

### Chapter 1, Form B

| | |
|---|---|
| 1. d | 11. F |
| 2. c | 12. T |
| 3. d | 13. F |
| 4. a | 14. T |
| 5. b | 15. T |
| 6. d | 16. F |
| 7. c | 17. F |
| 8. a | 18. F |
| 9. b | 19. T |
| 10. a | 20. F |

### Chapter 2, Form B

| | |
|---|---|
| 1. i | 14. F |
| 2. n | 15. T |
| 3. k | 16. T |
| 4. d | 17. T |
| 5. h | 18. T |
| 6. c | 19. F |
| 7. b | 20. F |
| 8. a | 21. T |
| 9. e | 22. T |
| 10. m | 23. F |
| 11. f | 24. T |
| 12. j | 25. T |
| 13. F | |

### Chapter 3, Form B

| | |
|---|---|
| 1. e | 11. T |
| 2. c | 12. T |
| 3. f | 13. T |
| 4. d | 14. T |
| 5. b | 15. F |
| 6. a | 16. F |
| 7. d | 17. F |
| 8. b | 18. T |
| 9. c | 19. F |
| 10. d | 20. T |

### Chapter 4, Form B

| | |
|---|---|
| 1. i | 14. a |
| 2. l | 15. d |
| 3. f | 16. F |
| 4. d | 17. F |
| 5. h | 18. T |
| 6. c | 19. F |
| 7. e | 20. T |
| 8. k | 21. F |
| 9. a | 22. T |
| 10. g | 23. T |
| 11. c | 24. T |
| 12. b | 25. F |
| 13. c | |

### Chapter 5, Form B

| | |
|---|---|
| 1. c | 21. EllisKandies |
| 2. d | 22. R |
| 3. a | 23. MacDonald |
| 4. f | 24. Roy |
| 5. e | 25. Slate |
| 6. 4 | 26. abc |
| 7. Larrys | 27. cba |
| 8. 9 | 28. cab |
| 9. Liz | 29. acb |
| 10. SixtyForty | 30. acb |
| 11. Dr | 31. bac |
| 12. 7 | 32. bca |
| 13. Claddock | 33. cab |
| 14. 98cent | 34. bac |
| 15. OReilly | 35. abc |
| 16. Wise | 36. cab |
| 17. deHinesto | 37. acb |
| 18. United | 38. cab |
| 19. Roasty | 39. acb |
| 20. Canada | 40. cab |

# Chapter 6, Form B

| | | | |
|---|---|---|---|
| 1. f | | 19. d | |
| 2. l | | 20. v | |
| 3. k | | 21. c | |
| 4. c | | 22. b | |
| 5. r | | 23. a | |
| 6. s | | 24. b | |
| 7. b | | 25. d | |
| 8. g | | 26. F | |
| 9. n | | 27. T | |
| 10. e | | 28. T | |
| 11. q | | 29. F | |
| 12. p | | 30. T | |
| 13. a | | 31. F | |
| 14. h | | 32. F | |
| 15. m | | 33. F | |
| 16. o | | 34. F | |
| 17. i | | 35. T | |
| 18. j | | | |

# Chapter 7, Form B

| | | |
|---|---|---|
| 1. d | 11. F |
| 2. j | 12. T |
| 3. g | 13. F |
| 4. a | 14. T |
| 5. k | 15. T |
| 6. f | 16. F |
| 7. l | 17. F |
| 8. i | 18. T |
| 9. e | 19. T |
| 10. b | 20. T |

# Chapter 8, Form B

| | | |
|---|---|---|
| 1. F | 14. e |
| 2. T | 15. j |
| 3. T | 16. g |
| 4. T | 17. h |
| 5. T | 18. k |
| 6. F | 19. c |
| 7. F | 20. i |
| 8. F | 21. a |
| 9. T | 22. c |
| 10. T | 23. d |
| 11. a | 24. c |
| 12. d | 25. c |
| 13. l | 26. b |

27. c
28. b
29. d
30. d
31. file name or full file name
32. output devices
33. filetype
34. shortcuts
35. floppy
36. criteria or requirements
37. digital signature
38. Find
39. application or program
40. number

# Chapter 9, Form B

| | | |
|---|---|---|
| 1. c | 24. T |
| 2. b | 25. F |
| 3. d | 26. c |
| 4. d | 27. c |
| 5. c | 28. a |
| 6. n | 29. a |
| 7. i | 30. f |
| 8. g | 31. e |
| 9. f | 32. h |
| 10. b | 33. c |
| 11. k | 34. b |
| 12. h | 35. h |
| 13. m | 36. h |
| 14. d | 37. b or g |
| 15. c | 38. c |
| 16. T | 39. d |
| 17. F | 40. f |
| 18. T | 41. c |
| 19. F | 42. b |
| 20. T | 43. c |
| 21. T | 44. c |
| 22. F | 45. a |
| 23. F | |

# Chapter 10, Form B

1. T
2. F
3. T
4. F
5. T
6. F
7. T
8. F
9. T
10. F
11. d
12. d
13. b
14. c
15. c
16. d
17. c
18. c
19. c
20. b
21. read
22. one of:
    console emulation,
    Telnet, or Remote
    Access Service
    (RAS)
23. top/sales/kentucky/
    oct.html
24. protocols
25. mapped drive
26. i
27. h
28. c
29. k
30. e
31. a
32. b
33. g
34. d
35. j
36. network media or
    media
37. domain name
38. client
39. gov
40. method or protocol

# Chapter 11, Form B

1. a
2. k
3. d
4. i
5. g
6. o
7. e
8. f
9. b
10. h
11. n
12. c
13. p
14. l
15. j
16. F
17. T
18. F
19. T
20. T
21. T
22. F
23. T
24. F
25. F
26. F
27. T
28. T
29. F
30. T
31. k
32. a
33. f
34. g
35. j
36. c
37. n
38. b
39. l
40. i
41. r
42. d
43. o
44. q
45. p
46. d
47. d
48. a
49. b
50. c

# Chapter 12, Form B

1. d
2. j
3. m
4. n
5. k
6. l
7. h
8. b
9. c
10. e
11. T
12. T
13. T
14. F
15. T
16. T
17. F
18. F
19. F
20. F
21. a
22. d
23. b
24. c
25. b
26. c
27. f
28. l
29. b
30. i
31. e
32. g
33. j
34. h
35. a

# KEY TO COMPREHENSIVE TEST, FORM A

## Chapters 1–12, Form A

| | | |
|---|---|---|
| 1. c | 39. a | 77. F |
| 2. c | 40. d | 78. F |
| 3. a | 41. T | 79. F |
| 4. a | 42. F | 80. T |
| 5. c | 43. T | 81. T |
| 6. d | 44. T | 82. T |
| 7. b | 45. T | 83. F |
| 8. c | 46. T | 84. T |
| 9. c | 47. F | 85. T |
| 10. b | 48. F | 86. T |
| 11. d | 49. F | 87. F |
| 12. b | 50. F | 88. T |
| 13. a | 51. T | 89. F |
| 14. b | 52. F | 90. T |
| 15. a | 53. T | 91. cab |
| 16. d | 54. T | 92. bac |
| 17. b | 55. T | 93. abc |
| 18. c | 56. T | 94. abc |
| 19. a | 57. F | 95. acb |
| 20. a | 58. F | 96. acb |
| 21. c | 59. F | 97. abc |
| 22. b | 60. T | 98. cab |
| 23. d | 61. T | 99. bac |
| 24. d | 62. F | 100. cba |
| 25. b | 63. F | |
| 26. b | 64. T | |
| 27. c | 65. T | |
| 28. b | 66. T | |
| 29. d | 67. F | |
| 30. d | 68. F | |
| 31. b | 69. F | |
| 32. b | 70. T | |
| 33. d | 71. T | |
| 34. b | 72. F | |
| 35. d | 73. F | |
| 36. c | 74. F | |
| 37. d | 75. T | |
| 38. a | 76. T | |

# KEY TO COMPREHENSIVE TEST, FORM B

## Chapters 1–12, Form B

| | | |
|---|---|---|
| 1. d | 39. c | 77. T |
| 2. a | 40. c | 78. T |
| 3. a | 41. T | 79. F |
| 4. d | 42. F | 80. T |
| 5. c | 43. T | 81. F |
| 6. d | 44. F | 82. F |
| 7. b | 45. T | 83. F |
| 8. d | 46. T | 84. F |
| 9. b | 47. T | 85. T |
| 10. b | 48. F | 86. T |
| 11. d | 49. T | 87. T |
| 12. d | 50. T | 88. T |
| 13. b | 51. T | 89. F |
| 14. c | 52. F | 90. T |
| 15. b | 53. F | 91. cba |
| 16. b | 54. F | 92. bac |
| 17. d | 55. T | 93. cab |
| 18. d | 56. T | 94. abc |
| 19. b | 57. F | 95. acb |
| 20. c | 58. F | 96. acb |
| 21. a | 59. F | 97. abc |
| 22. a | 60. T | 98. abc |
| 23. c | 61. T | 99. bac |
| 24. b | 62. F | 100. cab |
| 25. d | 63. F | |
| 26. a | 64. F | |
| 27. b | 65. T | |
| 28. a | 66. T | |
| 29. b | 67. T | |
| 30. d | 68. F | |
| 31. b | 69. F | |
| 32. c | 70. T | |
| 33. c | 71. T | |
| 34. b | 72. F | |
| 35. d | 73. F | |
| 36. c | 74. F | |
| 37. a | 75. T | |
| 38. a | 76. T | |

# CHAPTER TESTS, FORM A

# CHAPTER 1
## Introduction to Records and Information Management

## Objective Test—Form A

### Multiple Choice
In the blank after each item, write the letter of the best response. (5 points each, total 50)

1. An information system is a
   a. computer program to manage records.
   b. telephone system that can access records.
   c. way of planning, organizing, and developing information.
   d. set of books that describe how information is used.

   1. _____

2. If the cost of creating a record
   a. exceeds its value to the business, then it probably should not be created.
   b. is less than its value to the business, then it probably should not be created.
   c. exceeds its value to the business, then it probably should be destroyed.
   d. is less than its value to the business, then it probably should be destroyed.

   2. _____

3. Who is responsible for maintaining the integrity of an organization's records?
   a. The librarian
   b. The administrative assistant
   c. The records clerk
   d. The records and information manager

   3. _____

4. The records and information manager exercises records control within the organization by allowing access to records only to
   a. the organization's employees.
   b. authorized persons.
   c. the records clerk.
   d. the administrative assistant.

   4. _____

5. If a record cannot be found,
   a. it is documented as being lost.
   b. it has no value to the organization because it is not available for use.
   c. someone is assigned the job of reconstructing a similar record.
   d. someone is assigned the job of finding the record.

   5. _____

6. The records and information manager oversees the destruction of records when
   a. the organization is unable to locate or afford additional storage space.
   b. they are no longer needed in the operations of the organization.
   c. they are no longer required for legal reasons.
   d. they are no longer needed in the operations of the organization or required for legal reasons.

   6. _____

7. Records and information management professionals often have a      7. _____
   a. master's degree in accounting, finance, or economics.
   b. Ph.D. degree in one of the business disciplines or in information and library science.
   c. two- or four-year degree in business or information and library science.
   d. bachelor's degree in liberal arts, computer science, or environmental engineering.

8. The profession of records and information management consists of      8. _____
   a. two groups: specialists in RIM and those whose occupation includes the management of information but who have another specialty or job title.
   b. two groups: specialists in RIM and computer programmers.
   c. three groups: specialists in RIM, computer programmers, and those whose occupation includes the management of information but who have another specialty or job title.
   d. two groups: those whose occupation includes the management of information but who have another specialty or job title, and computer programmers.

9. A question that must be considered before a record is distributed is      9. _____
   a. How will the record be edited for accuracy?
   b. What medium will be used to create the record?
   c. How will the record be protected against disasters?
   d. How are copies to be sent to users?

10. Creation, distribution, maintenance, protection, control, storage, and destruction describe      10. _____
    a. the life cycle of records and information management.
    b. the duties of the records clerk.
    c. the functions of every business and organization.
    d. the duties of the administrative assistant.

## True or False

Circle T if the statement is true or F if the statement is false. (5 points each, total 50)

11. Destruction of records is part of the function of records and information management.      11. T F
12. Records management deals with paper records, whereas information management deals with computer records.      12. T F
13. Mail, fax machines, interoffice delivery, and electronic computer links are methods of distributing records to users.      13. T F
14. Maintaining the integrity of records means that they are kept in fireproof vaults at all times.      14. T F
15. Records should be protected from the hazards of fire and floods.      15. T F
16. *Filing* is the key word that should be considered in the storage function of RIM.      16. T F
17. Businesses do not have environmental protection policies because the government sets such policies.      17. T F
18. Records are stored and sometimes transferred to an inactive storage area once they are no longer in daily use.      18. T F
19. Office managers, administrative assistants, engineers, and accountants should have a college major in RIM.      19. T F
20. The primary responsibility of the professional records and information manager is to store records when they become inactive.      20. T F

# CHAPTER 2
## Employment in Records and Information Management

## Objective Test—Form A

### Matching
In the blank after each definition, write the letter of the term that best matches the definition. Not all of the terms will be used. (4 points each, total 48)

**Terms**

a. archival management

b. archives

c. archivist

d. ARMA International

e. certified records manager

f. consultant

g. educational records management

h. depository

i. ICRM

j. government records management

k. legal records management

l. medical records management

m. records center

n. SAA

**Definitions**

1. secure location dedicated to the storage of all types of records (usually part of the organization rather than a separate business)      1. _____

2. job title for a person who maintains archives      2. _____

3. acronym for a group of institutional members who are concerned with the identification, preservation, and use of records of historical value      3. _____

4. group of records, usually valuable and historical, that are not referred to on a daily basis for organizational operations      4. _____

5. secure location dedicated to the storage of all types of documents and records—usually a separate business      5. _____

6. a profession having to do with the management of legal records      6. _____

7. the leading professional organization for persons in the expanding field of records and information management      7. _____

8. maintaining a group of valuable records that are not referred to on a daily basis      8. _____

9. certifying organization of professional records managers and administrative officers who specialize in the field of records and information management      9. _____

10. person outside the organization who is hired to come into a business and make recommendations for more effective records systems      10. _____

11. a professional designation granted by the ICRM      11. _____

12. a records management specialty that includes local, state, and federal records      12. _____

# True or False

Circle T if the statement is true or F if the statement is false. (4 points each, total 52)

13. Hospitals, small manufacturers, and art retailers are examples of the types of organizations likely to employ archivists.  **13.**  T  F

14. A person who is responsible for ensuring the integrity of financial records has the duties of designing records systems, updating records, and designing controls.  **14.**  T  F

15. Wills, deeds, birth certificates, marriage records, and tax records are several types of legal records that might be kept by a governmental unit such as a city or county.  **15.**  T  F

16. Employees in medical RIM may have a background in business, medical technology, medical records, nursing, insurance, or health care services.  **16.**  T  F

17. In addition to storing and protecting records, depositories and records centers might also film records, destroy records, and recover records after a disaster.  **17.**  T  F

18. The use of professional RIM consultants is decreasing.  **18.**  T  F

19. One of the benefits ARMA members receive from the organization is discounts on filing equipment.  **19.**  T  F

20. The Institute of Certified Records Managers (ICRM) is the organization that oversees the professional designation of CRM.  **20.**  T  F

21. The financial records and information manager is more involved than the archivist with the daily operations of business.  **21.**  T  F

22. There are clearly defined categories of RIM specialties.  **22.**  T  F

23. One of the benefits of joining a professional organization is networking with other professionals to gather ideas and methods.  **23.**  T  F

24. The educational records management profession is often divided among local, state, and federal governments.  **24.**  T  F

25. Since the nature of records is changing as technology evolves, continued education for a records management professional is necessary.  **25.**  T  F

# CHAPTER 3
## Legal and Ethical Matters in Records and Information Management

## Objective Test—Form A

### Matching

In the blank after each definition, write the letter of the term that best matches the definition. Not all of the terms will be used. (5 points each, total 25)

**Terms**

    a. admissibility into evidence      d. criminal law
    b. civil law      e. litigation
    c. copyright      f. piracy

**Definitions**

1. statute covering a legal dispute between the government and an individual or business     1. _____

2. an exclusive entitlement granted by the government for the publication of an artistic, musical, or written work     2. _____

3. statute covering legal dispute between one individual or business and another     3. _____

4. to make illegal duplicates of copyrighted software     4. _____

5. to engage in a lawsuit     5. _____

### Multiple Choice

In the blank after each item, write the letter of the best response. (5 points each, total 25)

6. The source of information important to the government when determining whether or not a business is abiding by laws and regulations dealing with business is     6. _____
    a. archival records.
    b. all business records.
    c. active records.
    d. retention records.

7. The federal law that denies access to one's personal records without his or her permission is the     7. _____
    a. Federal Reports Act.
    b. Federal Records Act.
    c. Freedom of Information Act.
    d. Privacy Act.

8. An example of copyright infringement is     8. _____
    a. records destruction.
    b. price fixing.
    c. a civil dispute.
    d. software piracy.

9. Admissibility into evidence refers to whether or not          9. _____

    a. a photocopy, microfilm copy, or computer software copy of a document will be accepted in court as valid evidence in a lawsuit.

    b. the organization is responsible for gathering, organizing, and presenting its documents as evidence in a lawsuit.

    c. the court is responsible for gathering, organizing, and presenting the organization's documents as evidence in a lawsuit.

    d. the organization is permitted to destroy its documents after they have been presented in a lawsuit.

10. Examples of ethical business management are          10. _____

    a. low pay and few benefits for employees, straightforward advertising, and manufacture of safe products.

    b. fair pay and benefits for employees, straightforward advertising, and price fixing.

    c. fair pay and benefits for employees, straightforward advertising, and honest pricing.

    d. fair pay and benefits for employees, deceptive advertising, and manufacturing of safe products.

## True or False

Circle T if the statement is true or F if the statement is false. (5 points each, total 50)

| | | |
|---|---|---|
| **11.** It is important for records and information managers to be familiar with criminal and civil laws and regulations. | **11.** | T  F |
| **12.** The federal government allows state governments to determine whether or not citizens have the right to gain access to information about themselves. | **12.** | T  F |
| **13.** One may duplicate copyrighted items without permission of the owner if doing so for commercial use. | **13.** | T  F |
| **14.** It is important that RIM employees refrain from destroying records that might be relevant to a lawsuit. | **14.** | T  F |
| **15.** Legal action by the government for noncompliance is a risk the RIM manager must be aware of. | **15.** | T  F |
| **16.** Matters of business ethics have little relevance to the records and information management employee. | **16.** | T  F |
| **17.** Good ethical business management by the RIM can result in increased employee loyalty and productivity. | **17.** | T  F |
| **18.** Maintaining confidentiality of records is an example of how the RIM manager can observe high ethical standards. | **18.** | T  F |
| **19.** Bad morale is a likely result of straightforward advertising. | **19.** | T  F |
| **20.** Numerous local, state, and federal government laws and regulations have an impact upon how records and information are managed. | **20.** | T  F |

# CHAPTER 4
## Receipt and Creation of Hard Copy Records

# Objective Test—Form A

## Matching

In the blank after each definition, write the letter of the term that best matches the definition. Not all of the terms will be used. (4 points each, total 40)

**Terms**

| | |
|---|---|
| a. business forms | g. hard copy mail |
| b. discarded paperwork | h. incoming paperwork |
| c. e-mail | i. internal paperwork |
| d. fax | j. junk mail |
| e. form-filling software | k. outgoing paperwork |
| f. forms design software | l. voice mail |

**Definitions**

1. any kind of mail that arrives on paper
2. a means of sending a message or other document from one computer to one or more other computers
3. paperwork arriving from others outside the organization
4. a recorded message transmitted from one telephone to another
5. paper records with blank spaces to be filled in and that must be carefully managed and designed
6. paperwork going to others outside the organization
7. paperwork arriving from and departing to offices inside the organization
8. a reproduction of a document sent from one machine to another over telephone lines
9. computer software that helps in the design of efficient business forms
10. computer programs that enable us to fill in business forms using the computer printer instead of a typewriter

1. _____
2. _____
3. _____
4. _____
5. _____
6. _____
7. _____
8. _____
9. _____
10. _____

## Multiple Choice

In the blank after each item, write the letter of the best response. (4 points each, total 20)

11. The first step in opening the mail in a small organization is to:
    a. prioritize.
    b. organize.
    c. classify.
    d. open.

11. _____

12. To save paper when printing reports and other materials,                                                12. _____
    a. include headers at the top of each page.
    b. use larger left, right, top, and bottom margins.
    c. single-space and print on both sides of the paper.
    d. use a laser printer.

13. Detailed instructions on a business form should appear                                                  13. _____
    a. in the right margin.
    b. on the front.
    c. in the left margin.
    d. on the back.

14. Form-filling software is more efficient than filling out forms on a typewriter because it               14. _____
    a. allows a greater number of forms to be kept in storage.
    b. saves time by matching copy to be filled in with the blank spaces on the form.
    c. saves time by allowing the user to enter the information that is to appear on the paper form.
    d. allows the user to manipulate the design of the form.

15. To be classified as a record, a piece of paper must be                                                  15. _____
    a. less costly to the organization when thrown away than when kept.
    b. equal in cost to the organization when thrown away and when kept.
    c. more costly to the organization when thrown away than when kept.
    d. kept temporarily or discarded immediately.

## True or False
Circle T if the statement is true or F if the statement is false. (4 points each, total 40)

16. Developments in technology have made it less tempting to produce paperwork.            16.  T  F
17. Each incoming piece of paperwork is classified as a record to be kept.                 17.  T  F
18. Mail that comes in on paper is called hard copy mail.                                   18.  T  F
19. The volume of paper received and the size of the organization determine how incoming    19.  T  F
    paperwork is handled.
20. It is easy to determine the exact difference in the costs of keeping versus discarding   20.  T  F
    paperwork.
21. Records and information managers are responsible for thinking carefully prior to allowing   21.  T  F
    paperwork to be created.
22. Large-volume copying jobs should be done on site, especially in small businesses.       22.  T  F
23. Create a record only if it serves the organization and its clients or customers.        23.  T  F
24. When designing a business form, it is important to specify legal-size paper.            24.  T  F
25. It is important to keep track of who uses the copy machine and the number of copies made.   25.  T  F

# CHAPTER 5
## Indexing and Alphabetizing Procedures

## Objective Test—Form A

### Matching
In the blank after each definition, write the letter of the term that best matches the definition. Not all of the terms will be used. (3 points each, total 15)

**Terms**

a. alphabetizing        d. lowercase

b. case                 e. units

c. indexing             f. uppercase

**Definitions**

1. capital letters                                                                          1. _____
2. arranging in order according to the letters of the alphabet                              2. _____
3. determining the order and format of the units in a name when alphabetizing              3. _____
4. the name The Kozy Kiddie Korner, Inc., has five of these                                4. _____
5. small letters                                                                            5. _____

### Indexing
Write the *first indexing unit* of each name in the blank at the right. Omit any punctuation. The first item (0.) is an example. (2 points each, total 40)

0. New York Insurance Co.            0. New
6. Claude Eldon Slate                6. _____
7. Charlotte MacDonald               7. _____
8. Monty Ellis-Kandies               8. _____
9. The Roasty Toasty Grill           9. _____
10. Carlos de Hinesto                10. _____
11. Pat O'Reilly                     11. _____
12. Rev. Mary Claddock               12. _____
13. Dr. Wool Fashions                13. _____
14. "Liz" for Show, Inc.             14. _____
15. Larry's Electronic Repairs       15. _____
16. 4 on the Floor Transmission Repair  16. _____
17. 9th Avenue Cameras               17. _____
18. Sixty-Forty Trading Cards        18. _____
19. 7-6 Day Care, Ltd.               19. _____
20. The 98¢ Taco Hut                 20. _____
21. Police Dept., Wise, VA           21. _____
22. U.S. Dept. of State              22. _____
23. Wildlife Bureau, Canada          23. _____

**24.** R J Z Thrill Park                                   24. _____

**25.** Roy Rogers Restaurant                              25. _____

## Alphabetizing

In the blank at the right, indicate the alphabetic order of each name in the series of three names. The first item (0.) is an example. (3 points each, total 45)

**0.** (a) Louis Pryor; (b) Lois Pryor; (c) M. Prime                                    **0.** cba

**26.** (a) W. Allen Brown; (b) Brown-Young Pharmacists; (c) Bryan Brown              **26.** _____

**27.** (a) West-Berry, Inc.; (b) Western Laundromat; (c) West and Brill, Inc.        **27.** _____

**28.** (a) Chas. Wilt Co.; (b) Cecil Wilson; (c) Charley Wilt, Inc.                  **28.** _____

**29.** (a) Wm. Scully; (b) Willard Scolly; (c) W. O. Scully-Weston                   **29.** _____

**30.** (a) Merino's Check Cashing Service; (b) Cora Marino; (c) Consuelo Meriam, Jr.  **30.** _____

**31.** (a) 1-2-3 Computer College; (b) One for Your Money Hair Salon; (c) 1-Fine Time Travel  **31.** _____
Service

**32.** (a) Bud & Sam Candies; (b) Bud Answering Service; (c) The Bud and Rose Flower Shop  **32.** _____

**33.** (a) 4th Street Bonding Co.; (b) 4 Your Wedding Accessories; (c) 40 Mile Beach Hotel  **33.** _____

**34.** (a) Public Schools, City of Alberta; (b) Alberta Door Mfg. Co.; (c) Alberta Classroom  **34.** _____
Supplies

**35.** (a) Dalton Co., 226 Moyer Ave., Oakland, CA; (b) Dalton Co., Massey Dr., Oxnard, CA;  **35.** _____
(c) Dalton Co., 12472 Moyer Ave., Oakland, CA

**36.** (a) U.S. Dept. of Justice; (b) United States Gypsum Co.; (c) United Stay-Fast Co.  **36.** _____

**37.** (a) The Carriage House; (b) Carriage of Contentment, Inc.; (c) Carriage by Nicholas, Ltd.  **37.** _____

**38.** (a) Alice Beckerman; (b) Bank of the Southwest; (c) Beck's Studios           **38.** _____

**39.** (a) Kazan Bierominello; (b) Karen Beironnello; (c) Kastas Bieromnellio        **39.** _____

**40.** (a) The O'Briens' Shop; (b) Sophia O'Brien; (c) Shirley O'Brian              **40.** _____

# CHAPTER 6
## Systems for Organizing Paper Records

## Objective Test—Form A

### Matching

In the blank after each definition, write the letter of the term that best matches the definition. Not all of the terms will be used. (3 points each, total 60)

**Terms**

a. ADA
b. alphabetic
c. chronological
d. cross-reference
e. cut
f. dictionary
g. ELF
h. encyclopedic

i. ergonomics
j. file folder
k. file guide
l. file label
m. filing equipment
n. filing supplies
o. geographic
p. indirect

q. numeric
r. subject
s. subject-numeric
t. system entry
u. system storage
v. tab

**Definitions**

1. a notation that a record is filed in another location                                              1. _____
2. the applied science of conforming equipment, systems, and the working environment to the requirements of people, including those who have disabilities                                              2. _____
3. consists primarily of file containers and cabinets and filing accessories                                              3. _____
4. legislation that includes requirements for accessibility to equipment by persons who have disabilities                                              4. _____
5. system for organizing records according to preassigned or assigned numbers                                              5. _____
6. file folders and pockets for paper records and accessories such as file dividers and labels                                              6. _____
7. system for organizing records according to the sequence of letters in the alphabet                                              7. _____
8. system for organizing records by topic                                              8. _____
9. cardboard divider used to support folders and identify file sections                                              9. _____
10. arrangement of files in alphabetic order by subject captions with no subheadings                                              10. _____
11. an extension at the top of a folder or guide where a label is placed for identification                                              11. _____
12. a heavy paper container for filed records                                              12. _____
13. system for organizing records by locality, area, or territory                                              13. _____
14. alphabetic arrangement of records by subject captions with headings and subheadings                                              14. _____
15. any filing system that requires reference to an index before the records can be located                                              15. _____
16. the width of a folder or guide tab relative to the width of the folder or guide                                              16. _____
17. a campaign by ARMA to eliminate legal-size files and legal-size paper                                              17. _____
18. similar to encyclopedic subject systems except that numbers are used to identify the captions                                              18. _____
19. system for organizing records by date                                              19. _____
20. small adhesive tag used to identify folders and guides                                              20. _____

## Multiple Choice

In the blank after each item, write the letter of the best response. (4 points each, total 20)

21. The purpose of a file guide is to
    a. contain significant correspondence arranged in order by number.
    b. support file folders and to label major sections of the file.
    c. identify the location, area, or territory of the file equipment.
    d. contain significant correspondence arranged in order by date.

    21. _____

22. ADA stands for
    a. Americans with Disabilities Act.
    b. American Disabilities Association.
    c. American Database Association.
    d. Association for Directors of America.

    22. _____

23. A letter book contains correspondence in order by
    a. subject and number.
    b. subject.
    c. number.
    d. date.

    23. _____

24. Records should be stored inside a file folder with the front facing the user and the heading to the
    a. right.
    b. left.
    c. top.
    d. bottom.

    24. _____

25. The best candidates for subject filing are
    a. numbered forms such as invoices, requisitions, and checks.
    b. employee records such as applications for employment and pay records.
    c. records that refer to products, processes, and formulas.
    d. records that refer to locality, area, or sales territory.

    25. _____

## True or False

Circle T if the statement is true or F if the statement is false. (2 points each, total 20)

26. Motorized files are less expensive to purchase and repair than are manually operated equipment.  26. T F
27. Ergonomic factors include geographic, subject, and numeric filing of records.  27. T F
28. Legal-size files and paper are more costly than standard-size equipment and paper.  28. T F
29. Additional floor space is one example of an extra cost associated with using paper records systems.  29. T F
30. Lawyers, physicians, and dentists will most likely arrange their client and patient folders in order by subject.  30. T F
31. Labels for folders and guides can be printed from a computer database or keyed on a typewriter.  31. T F
32. The storage documentation step is mandatory for both large-scale and small-scale systems.  32. T F
33. Subject-numeric files are similar to dictionary subject files except that numbers are used to identify the captions.  33. T F
34. A sales business with definite geographic sales areas would be likely to organize certain records geographically by sales territory.  34. T F
35. Numeric filing is a direct system.  35. T F

# CHAPTER 7
## Retrieval, Retention, and Recycling

## Objective Test—Form A

### Matching
In the blank after each definition, write the letter of the term that best matches the definition. Not all of the terms will be used. (5 points each, total 50)

**Terms**

| | | |
|---|---|---|
| a. by-product information | e. network | i. recycle |
| b. disintegrator | f. out guide | j. requisition |
| c. electronic access | g. pulping | k. retention |
| d. incinerate | h. recovery | l. retention schedule |

**Definitions**

1. a machine that chops materials into small pieces                                          1. _____
2. a group of computers linked electronically                                                 2. _____
3. to manufacture paper and other products from waste, scrap, used paper, and other items     3. _____
4. a form that lists each type of record and the number of years each is to be retained       4. _____
5. a heavy paper signpost that documents the location from which a record was removed, the
   name of the record, the borrower, and the date                                             5. _____
6. the period of time that records are kept or retained                                       6. _____
7. a group of facts created for a secondary reason                                            7. _____
8. a process used to destroy records by adding water and creating a slurry mixture            8. _____
9. a written request for records                                                              9. _____
10. to destroy records by burning them                                                        10. _____

### True or False
Circle T if the statement is true or F if the statement is false. (5 points each, total 50)

11. The three Rs of records and information management are retrieval, retention, and recycling.    **11.** T  F
12. Cost is one of the five major components in the retrieval function.                            **12.** T  F
13. Electronic access to records has become the norm in recent years.                              **13.** T  F
14. In the delivery component of retrieval, records are delivered to a records storage area to be filed.  **14.** T  F
15. The primary purpose of the documentation component of retrieval is to make a record of         **15.** T  F
    where documents are filed.
16. Follow-up is the component of retrieval in which records employees communicate with users if   **16.** T  F
    borrowed records are due.
17. Records retention is probably the most complex and difficult issue that the professional records  **17.** T  F
    and information manager must address.
18. Federal, state, and local governments allow organizations to use their own discretion when     **18.** T  F
    making decisions about keeping or destroying records.
19. A precise retention schedule can be one result of a well-planned retention policy.             **19.** T  F
20. Three major considerations in destroying records are cost, security, and environmental protection.  **20.** T  F

# CHAPTER 8
## Managing Electronic Files

# Objective Test—Form A

## Multiple Choice
In the blank after each item, write the letter of the best response. (3 points each, total 30)

**1.** A backup that includes only files that changed since the last backup is called a(n)     1. _____
   a. incomplete backup.
   b. change backup.
   c. full backup.
   d. incremental backup.

**2.** A file name called *JohnHarrison is a \*.doc* is not a legal file name in MS Windows because it     2. _____
   a. has too many characters.
   b. contains spaces.
   c. contains a *.
   d. does not use numbers.

**3.** The following are storage devices except     3. _____
   a. the floppy disk.
   b. the CD-ROM.
   c. the CPU.
   d. tape.

**4.** In the file called *MyFile.txt*, the characters *txt* are the     4. _____
   a. filetype.
   b. association.
   c. abbreviation.
   d. file name.

**5.** An electronic file drawer that is accessed directly using a drive letter is called the     5. _____
   a. top folder.
   b. main folder.
   c. prime directory.
   d. root directory.

**6.** The following are examples of metadata except     6. _____
   a. the creation date.
   b. keywords.
   c. the C: drive.
   d. the file size.

7. The set of requirements that make up a search for electronic records is called

    a. the search pattern.

    b. search rules.

    c. criteria.

    d. the methodology.

7. _____

8. The electronic equivalent of a file drawer that contains multiple documents is a

    a. multi-store.

    b. directory.

    c. shortcut.

    d. filing space.

8. _____

9. The one program that is required for the computer to function is the

    a. CPU.

    b. word processor.

    c. calculator program.

    d. operating system.

9. _____

10. The following principles should be followed when naming files except

    a. identification.

    b. grammatical correctness.

    c. brevity.

    d. documentation.

10. _____

# Matching

In the blank after each definition, write the letter of the term that best matches the definition. Not all of the terms will be used. (2 points each, total 20)

**Terms**

| | | |
|---|---|---|
| a. application | e. digital | i. metadata |
| b. association | f. file | j. operating system |
| c. byte | g. file system | k. shortcut |
| d. CPU | h. hardware | l. storage device |

**Definitions**

11. where a single character is stored on a computer ............................ 11. _____

12. the brain of the computer ............................ 12. _____

13. the physical parts of a computer, such as the CPU and monitor ............................ 13. _____

14. the computer's hard drive is an example ............................ 14. _____

15. computers that manipulate numbers ............................ 15. _____

16. a program that manages the computer's hardware and acts as a manager of other programs ............................ 16. _____

17. a set of folders and files set up as a hierarchical means to store electronic records on the computer ............................ 17. _____

18. a file that contains instructions for creating or manipulating electronic records ............................ 18. _____

19. a special file used only for telling the operating system the location of another file ............................ 19. _____

20. information about the contents of a file ............................ 20. _____

# True or False

Circle T if the statement is true or F if the statement is false (2 points each, total 20)

21. A folder can contain files but not other folders.                                     21.  T  F
22. The file type should not be changed.                                                  22.  T  F
23. The subject of a Microsoft Office document is part of the metadata.                    23.  T  F
24. The D drive is typically a hard drive.                                                 24.  T  F
25. Folder names in Windows 95 can have only twenty characters.                            25.  T  F
26. *Find* can locate files based on text known to exist in the document.                  26.  T  F
27. When sending an electronic document to a customer, the file name should include the    27.  T  F
    document tracking number.
28. Tapes and CD-R discs can be used to create file system backups.                        28.  T  F
29. A missing file can always be retrieved from the last incremental backup tape.          29.  T  F
30. The operating system is used to manage your appointments.                              30.  T  F

# Short Answer

In the blank after each definition, write the term that best matches the definition. (3 points each, total 30)

31. The part of a document name that allows the operating system to         31. _____
    associate a program is called the _____.

32. The MS Windows operating systems provide a file search                  32. _____
    tool called _____.

33. Multiple filing methodologies can be implemented with the same          33. _____
    electronic records by using _____.

34. The **A** drive in a Windows computer must be a                         34. _____
    _____ drive.

35. The set of electronic instructions that computers use to create         35. _____
    and manipulate other electronic documents is called
    a(n) _____.

36. The monitor, printer, and speakers are all called _____.           36. _____

37. The advanced search feature of Microsoft Office allows the user         37. _____
    to find files based on specific _____.

38. An outside recipient can verify the source of an electronic docu-       38. _____
    ment if you include a _____.

39. In a digital computer, the character z is represented with              39. _____
    a(n) _____.

40. When printing electronic documents, you should include the              40. _____
    _____ as part of the header or footer so that others can
    find the electronic version.

# CHAPTER 9
## Using Electronic Databases

## Objective Test—Form A

### Matching I

In the blank after each definition, write the letter of the term that best matches the definition. Not all of the terms will be used. (2 points each, total 20)

**Terms**

| | | |
|---|---|---|
| a. dbms | f. normalization | k. record |
| b. field | g. numeric | l. report |
| c. form | h. object | m. string |
| d. key | i. query | n. table |
| e. memo | j. rdbms | |

**Definitions**

1. the structure that stores data for multiple entries                                                1. _____
2. often used for entry and one-record-at-a-time viewing of database information      2. _____
3. a field that should be used for storage whenever mathematical calculations are used on data   3. _____
4. the process of splitting information into multiple related tables so that pieces of data are not repeated   4. _____
5. where a single piece of information (like a phone number) is stored                       5. _____
6. where multiple pieces of information, related to a single item or activity, are stored   6. _____
7. a question that you ask the database                                                                  7. _____
8. because of particular sorting requirements, it is best to store a zip code as this      8. _____
9. a piece of information that is considered unique and is used to identify an item or activity   9. _____
10. pictures, files, and other large pieces of data are stored as this in the database   10. _____

### Multiple Choice I

In the blank after each item, write the letter of the best response. (3 points each, total 15)

11. A field used to store only a limited number of known values is usually created as a
    a. short string.                                                                                          11. _____
    b. limited string.
    c. list.
    d. number.

12. A table is created to hold the names and addresses of all customers. A second table is
    created to hold all product orders. The two tables are then connected using a           12. _____
    a. link.
    b. shortcut.
    c. tether.
    d. relation.

**13.** In the example in question 12, people can view the connected tables because records in each of the tables have a special field containing identical values. This field is called a(n)

    a. tag.

    b. key.

    c. ID.

    d. connector.

13. _____

**14.** In a query, the rules that determine which information is displayed are called

    a. query rules.

    b. questions.

    c. criteria.

    d. requests.

14. _____

**15.** The process of deciding how to divide fields into related tables to remove duplication is called

    a. bisecting.

    b. relating.

    c. linking.

    d. normalization.

15. _____

## Multiple Choice II

In the blank after each item, write the letter of the string size that is most appropriate for the field. The majority of entries will fit with a minimum waste of space. (3 points each, total 15)

**16.** A zip code (e.g., 11234-5679)

    (a) 30    (b) 10    (c) 5    (d) 9

16. _____

**17.** United States Postal Service abbreviations for U.S. states

    (a) 2    (b) 6    (c) 25    (d) 13

17. _____

**18.** Personal title (e.g., Mr., Ms., etc.)

    (a) 1    (b) 2    (c) 4    (d) 10

18. _____

**19.** Month of the year (e.g., January)

    (a) 4    (b) 3    (c) 9    (d) 12

19. _____

**20.** Street name (e.g., First St.)

    (a) 5    (b) 10    (c) 25    (d) 100

20. _____

## True or False

Circle T if the statement is true or F if the statement is false. (2 points each, total 20)

**21.** Information can be stored only in tables.    21. T F

**22.** Records are stored in a table in alphabetical order.    22. T F

**23.** A key field in two or more tables is used to create a relation.    23. T F

**24.** A field can store a string and a number simultaneously.    24. T F

**25.** A list is used when a field can have only a few specific values.    25. T F

**26.** Forms exist only to help the user enter and view information in the database.    26. T F

27. Normalization usually increases the amount of information in the database.  **27.** T F
28. Queries are the primary means of entering information into the database.  **28.** T F
29. Pictures, videos, and other nonstandard information can be stored in a database as an object.  **29.** T F
30. Searching for documents on the Web can be accomplished only using mathematical equations.  **30.** T F

# Matching II

In the blank after each field definition, write the letter of the field type that is most appropriate for the information to be stored. (2 points each, total 30)

**Field Types**

    a. date                     d. logical                 g. object

    b. link                     e. memo                h. string

    c. list                      f. number

**Field Name: Description**

Questions 31–38 are fields in a hospital's patient database.

31. Birthdate: the month/day/year of birth     **31.** _____
32. Bloodtype: A, B, AB, or O     **32.** _____
33. RHFactor: + or −     **33.** _____
34. TimeIn: the time of day the patient was checked in     **34.** _____
35. MaritalStatus: Single, Married, Divorced, Widowed, or Separated     **35.** _____
36. Symptoms: description of symptoms as relayed by the patient (should handle three paragraphs)     **36.** _____
37. Insurer: name of the insurance company     **37.** _____
38. Total Cost: sum of the room charge, medicine charge, labor, and taxes     **38.** _____

Questions 39–45 are fields in an online bookseller's database.

39. BookTitle: the formal title of the book     **39.** _____
40. CustomerID: used as the customer table key field     **40.** _____
41. BookCover: an image of the book cover     **41.** _____
42. Genre: one of a predefined set of strings such as Mystery or Comedy     **42.** _____
43. Hardback: true if the book is a hardback     **43.** _____
44. ISBN: the book's identification number in the Library of Congress (must look like 1-55812-306-9)     **44.** _____
45. Review: location of file containing book review     **45.** _____

# CHAPTER 10
## Network-Based Records Management

## Objective Test—Form A

### Multiple Choice
In the blank after each item, write the letter of the best response. (3 points each, total 30)

1. The domain name *wlu.edu* is the Internet site for a
   a. high school.
   b. college or university.
   c. large electronics company.
   d. vocational learning center.

   1. _____

2. In a computer network, a protocol is
   a. a special piece of computer hardware for accessing the network.
   b. what is used when you write your e-mail message to the boss.
   c. a new technology for downloading Web pages quickly.
   d. a set of rules and codes that allow computers to communicate with each other.

   2. _____

3. *Larrysmith@majorcorp.com* is a(n)
   a. Web page.
   b. small computer at the MajorCorp company.
   c. e-mail address.
   d. shortcut to a shared folder.

   3. _____

4. The following are all network equipment except the
   a. hub.
   b. router.
   c. switch.
   d. scanner.

   4. _____

5. All computers that operate on a network must have a(n)
   a. server license.
   b. e-mail account.
   c. address.
   d. monitor.

   5. _____

6. All of the following are valid file permissions except
   a. read.
   b. change.
   c. authorize.
   d. none of the above.

   6. _____

**7.** A computer using Windows 3.1 would see a shared file name called
*JohnHarrison.letter.doc* as

    a. $JOHN1%@sdf@#$

    b. JohnHarr.letter

    c. JohnHarrison.letter.doc

    d. JOHNHA ~ 1.DOC

**7.** _____

**8.** The following designations are all top-level domains except

    a. com

    b. edu

    c. dell

    d. us

**8.** _____

**9.** A shared folder can be accessed by

    a. computers anywhere on the Internet.

    b. people with a valid e-mail address.

    c. computers using the same LAN.

    d. Web servers.

**9.** _____

**10.** A domain name allows computers on the Internet

    a. to secure their documents.

    b. to be uniquely identified.

    c. to violate network protocols.

    d. to control other computers.

**10.** _____

## Matching

In the blank after each definition, write the letter of the term that best matches the definition. Not all of the terms will be used. (2 points each, total 20)

**Terms**

| | | |
|---|---|---|
| a. domain name | e. LAN | i. protocol |
| b. e-mail | f. modem | j. server |
| c. ethernet | g. path | k. shared |
| d. Internet | h. peer | l. top-level domain |

**Definitions**

**11.** a computer that both requests information from and provides information to another computer

**11.** _____

**12.** a type of cable used as network media, to carry electronic information from computer to computer

**12.** _____

**13.** the network media, protocols, and equipment located within a single office or business

**13.** _____

**14.** a message sent from one person to another across a network

**14.** _____

**15.** the part of an Internet document address that includes the computer, folders, and file name

**15.** _____

**16.** a set of electronic codes that computers on the network all understand and that allows them to start a communication

**16.** _____

**17.** a network of networks that connects many LANs together so that messages and documents can be sent from one network to another

**17.** _____

**18.** the name of a computer used as a Web address on the Internet (e.g., *www.companyname.com*)

**18.** _____

**19.** a computer whose job is to wait for a request for an electronic document and send it to the requesting computer

19. _____

**20.** a folder on your computer that allows other computers on the network to access it

20. _____

## True or False
Circle T if the statement is true or F if the statement is false (2 points each, total 20)

**21.** A shared folder can be accessed by anyone on the Internet.  
21. T F

**22.** A TLD can be an organizational designation or a country code.  
22. T F

**23.** Computers on a network must all have a unique address.  
23. T F

**24.** A file server requests files from other computers.  
24. T F

**25.** A person with *read* access to a network document cannot modify it.  
25. T F

**26.** A folder's share name must be the same as its computer name.  
26. T F

**27.** A Web browser is software that acts as a client on the network.  
27. T F

**28.** Network equipment is used to ensure that a message gets from one computer to another.  
28. T F

**29.** Hyperlinks increase the speed of your LAN cables.  
29. T F

**30.** Searching for documents on the Web can only be accomplished using mathematical equations.  
30. T F

## Short Answer
In the blank after each definition, write the term that best matches the definition. (3 points each, total 30)

**31.** The U.S. Senate, IRS, National Institutes of Health, and NASA all have a top-level domain (TLD) of _____.

31. _____

**32.** A person who can view a file in a shared folder but not make changes to it has _____ access to that folder.

32. _____

**33.** In the URL *http://www.abc.com/top/sales/kentucky/oct.html*, the relative path of the document is _____.

33. _____

**34.** Access to a file server can be made in an MS Windows environment using the Network Neighborhood, or by making it appear that another disk is available by creating a(n) _____.

34. _____

**35.** The set of electronic codes that allows computers to communicate with each other on a network is called _____.

35. _____

**36.** The wires or fiber-optic cable or radio waves that carry information on a network are _____.

36. _____

**37.** One of the methods of accessing shared folders and drives from a remote location is _____.

37. _____

**38.** In the URL *http://www.abc.com/top/sales/kentucky/oct.html*, the characters *www.abc.com* are called the _____.

38. _____

**39.** A computer (or program) that usually requests information from other computers (or programs) on a network is called a(n) _____.

39. _____

**40.** In the URL *http://www.abc.com/top/sales/kentucky/oct.html*, the characters *http:* are called the _____.

40. _____

# CHAPTER 11
## Image Technology and Automated Systems

## Objective Test—Form A

### Matching I
In the blank after each definition, write the letter of the term that best matches the definition. Not all of the terms will be used. (2 points each, total 30)

**Terms**

a. bar code
b. CD-R
c. CD-RW
d. data image
e. disk technology
f. DVD
g. image scanner
h. image technology

i. microfiche
j. microfilm
k. microfilmer
l. microform or microrecord
m. optical character recognition
n. reader or viewer
o. real image
p. redundancy

**Definitions**

1. a 16-mm, 35-mm, or 105-mm roll of film containing microforms

1. _____

2. duplication

2. _____

3. a machine that magnifies the miniature images of a microform and displays them on a screen

3. _____

4. compact disk-recordable; a relatively inexpensive compact disk onto which data can be recorded once

4. _____

5. the use of computer disks to store real images

5. _____

6. a machine into which paper documents are fed for conversion to electronic form, usually onto one of several types of disks

6. _____

7. information, rather than a picture, that is captured from paper and converted to electronic form

7. _____

8. pattern of bars, or lines, that have a unique meaning and represent a single document or file

8. _____

9. a miniature picture of a single paper record on a microfilm roll or microfiche

9. _____

10. compact disk-rewritable; a compact disk onto which new data can be recorded over old data

10. _____

11. the conversion of paper records to photographic or electronic form and the administration of the new form

11. _____

12. digital video disk; an emerging technology that may replace conventional compact disk technology

12. _____

13. an exact reproduction on film or in electronic form of a paper record

14. a flat, transparent film sheet containing microforms

13. _____

15. a camera specially designed to take the pictures of documents onto microfilm or microfiche

14. _____

15. _____

# True or False

Circle T if the statement is true or F if the statement is false. (2 points each, total 30)

| | | |
|---|---|---|
| 16. Both microfilm and microfiche are microrecords. | 16. | T F |
| 17. CD-RW and CD-R are both inexpensive disks. | 17. | T F |
| 18. Micrographic technology greatly reduces the cost of storage space. | 18. | T F |
| 19. Image scanning technology is newer than micrographic technology. | 19. | T F |
| 20. In the term RAID, the letters RA mean "read access." | 20. | T F |
| 21. DVD technology is gradually being phased out. | 21. | T F |
| 22. With CD-R disks, you can erase but not record information. | 22. | T F |
| 23. Bar codes are read by scanners. | 23. | T F |
| 24. The U.S. Postal Service has yet to adopt bar-coding technology. | 24. | T F |
| 25. Although the initial installation of a bar-coding system is expensive, it can pay for itself in as little as one year. | 25. | T F |
| 26. Automated records management systems are software programs that make files, documents, and other records accessible for management by computer. | 26. | T F |
| 27. Both conventional and imaging (full-text) automated records management systems require computer software. | 27. | T F |
| 28. MICR technology is used primarily in the insurance industry. | 28. | T F |
| 29. Three major considerations in choosing an automated records management system are functions, cost, and architecture. | 29. | T F |
| 30. When selecting an automated records management system, architecture should be decided on before other factors are considered. | 30. | T F |

# Matching II

In the blank after each definition, write the letter of the term that best matches the definition. Not all of the terms will be used. (2 points each, total 30)

### Terms

| | | |
|---|---|---|
| a. architecture | g. command-driven | m. menu-driven |
| b. background processes | h. conventional | n. phrase search |
| c. batch processes | i. global modification | o. reservation |
| d. Boolean logic search | j. GUI | p. toggle |
| e. charge back | k. icon | q. waiting list |
| f. charge-out and return | l. keyword search | r. wild card search |

### Definitions

31. feature that enables the user to switch between one program and another without exiting either — 31. _____

32. query using more than one keyword or phrase and a logic statement (*AND, OR, NOT, EXCEPT, IF, THEN*) to limit or expand the scope of the search — 32. _____

33. addition or deletion made throughout a system with a single command — 33. _____

34. a systems feature that permits processes such as queries and indexing to be executed while the user performs other functions within the program — 34. _____

35. a system feature in which a group of records can all be processed at one time — 35. _____

36. system operation method in which the user must enter keywords or instructions — 36. _____

37. characteristics of hardware and software used in an automated system — 37. _____

38. screen picture selected by a mouse to operate a system that is menu-driven — 38. _____

39. to document the loan of an item and note its return — 39. _____

**40.** feature that enables the user to select screen options and operate the system with a keyboard, a mouse, or other input device, and uses graphic images, windows, forms, and icons

**40.** _____

**41.** using two or more consecutive words in a field to find a record

**41.** _____

**42.** using any single word in a field to find a record

**42.** _____

**43.** to use a symbol, such as * or ?, to look for records when some of the information is missing

**43.** _____

**44.** request-handling feature that enables an item to be held for delivery on a specified date

**44.** _____

**45.** feature that places a potential user on a list for records that have been charged out

**45.** _____

## Multiple Choice

In the blank after each item, write the letter of the best response. (2 points each, total 10)

**46.** Major functions of automated records management systems include all of the following except management of

**46.** _____

    a. records center employees.

    b. all types of active records.

    c. records for a specific industry.

    d. records retention.

**47.** Menu-driven systems

**47.** _____

    a. require entry of keywords or instructions.

    b. are used primarily in the restaurant industry.

    c. permit the user to select from a list of choices.

    d. require a menu driver to boot the system.

**48.** Total costs for an automated records management system consist of

**48.** _____

    a. overhead, such as costs of heat and electricity.

    b. initial outlay, maintenance, support, and training.

    c. the amount paid for the system software and hardware.

    d. salaries of those operating the system.

**49.** Container management refers to

**49.** _____

    a. controlling active and inactive records in a central location.

    b. containing costs in the operation of automated records management systems.

    c. delivering records to users in approved file boxes and other containers.

    d. reserving space for and monitoring the contents of file containers.

**50.** Factors considered in the architecture of an automated records management system include the

**50.** _____

    a. quality of the software being purchased.

    b. management functions that the system will perform.

    c. total cost of the automated system.

    d. types of computers on which the software will run.

# CHAPTER 12
## Safety, Security, and Disaster Recovery

## Objective Test—Form A

### Matching I

In the blank after each definition, write the letter of the term that best matches the definition. Not all of the terms will be used. (3 points each, total 30)

**Terms**

a. authentication
b. battery backup
c. carpal tunnel syndrome
d. electronic vaulting
e. facial recognition
f. fingerprint scanner
g. human disaster

h. integrated security system
i. natural disaster
j. password
k. smart card
l. sprinkler system
m. surge protector
n. voice-input computer

**Definitions**

1. type of biometric access control device that reads the characteristics of a person's face                                    1. _____
2. computer and software that enable the user to speak into a microphone to enter data into a computer system                       2. _____
3. the identification code used as part of an authentication system                                                                 3. _____
4. series of devices that spray water automatically when excess heat is sensed                                                      4. _____
5. an injury to the wrist that can be caused by the repetitive motions of working at a computer keyboard                            5. _____
6. small microprocessor used for access to a storage area                                                                           6. _____
7. system that provides standby power to a computer system in case of a temporary loss of electrical power                          7. _____
8. a unit between the computer power cord and the electrical outlet that can calm electrical current overloads and thus prevent the destruction of data   8. _____
9. methods of controlling access to facilities such as office buildings, floors, and rooms                                          9. _____
10. service of storing backup copies of vital electronic records                                                                    10. _____

### True or False

Circle T if the statement is true or F if the statement is false. (2 points each, total 20)

11. The use of an ergonomic keyboard should be considered as one way to reduce repetitive motion injuries.                    11.  T  F
12. Companies use a firewall to scramble and unscramble data sent over the Internet.                                          12.  T  F
13. The RIM should consider the costs prior to the selection of a records security system.                                    13.  T  F
14. Unlike paper records, records stored in electronic databases are free from possible destruction.                          14.  T  F
15. A records manager cannot prevent human disasters from happening.                                                          15.  T  F

16. Equipment and buildings have improved, resulting in disaster preparedness becoming somewhat less important in recent years.                16.   T   F

17. A nuclear accident is a human disaster.                17.   T   F

18. Many records can be saved after being exposed to the heat, smoke, and flames of a serious fire.                18.   T   F

19. Paper documents exposed to water damage can often be restored by using one of the drying techniques.                19.   T   F

20. When recovering wet paper, take immediate action to avoid the accumulation of mold.                20.   T   F

## Multiple Choice
In the blank after each item, write the letter of the best response. (4 points each, total 20)

21. The first step in avoiding injuries in records areas is to                21. _____
   a. avoid overloading electrical circuits.
   b. avoid tripping over electrical cords on walkways.
   c. speak to the records workers about safety precautions.
   d. develop a written, comprehensive safety plan.

22. Records security measures protect records from different types of risks such as                22. _____
   a. improper access, accidental loss, theft, damage, and unwanted destruction.
   b. misplacing the records and not organizing the records in proper order within file drawers.
   c. electrical circuit overload, file tipping, and collisions.
   d. carpal tunnel syndrome, electrical circuit overload, and misplacing records within file drawers.

23. Biometric access control devices can evaluate the physical characteristics of a person's                23. _____
   a. weight.
   b. heartbeat.
   c. eyes.
   d. height.

24. The purpose of an authentication system is to                24. _____
   a. avoid the misplacement of paper records and computer data.
   b. protect the data in a computer or computer network by controlling user access.
   c. protect and control the access to facilities such as office buildings, floors, and rooms.
   d. prevent paper record damage by converting printed text and graphics to computer data.

25. According to Chapter 12, UPS stands for                25. _____
   a. United Parcel Service
   b. uninterruptible power source
   c. uninterruptible password system
   d. unidentified password security

# Matching II

In the blank after each definition, write the letter of the term that best matches the definition. Not all of the terms will be used. (3 points each, total 30)

## Terms

a. air drying
b. black box
c. computer virus
d. detector
e. disaster recovery
f. electronic key

g. electronic security card
h. freeze drying
i. repetitive motion injury
j. scanner
k. UPS
l. voice-activated

## Definitions

26. unwanted program instructions that can alter and destroy data

26. _____

27. electronic access control plastic passkey without the grooves of traditional keys

27. _____

28. biometric access control system that reads voice patterns

28. _____

29. technology that uses a communication security device containing information about authorized users

29. _____

30. damage to nerves and muscles caused by repetitive movement

30. _____

31. executing plans for saving as many records as possible after a disaster

31. _____

32. electronic control access device that looks like a credit card, with a magnetic strip on one side

32. _____

33. input device that converts printed text and graphics to computer data

33. _____

34. technique for removing water from soaked records by first freezing them and then allowing the ice to melt and evaporate

34. _____

35. technique for removing water from soaked documents by placing them on polyester webbing and allowing the water to evaporate

35. _____

# CHAPTER TESTS, FORM B

# CHAPTER 1
## Introduction to Records and Information Management

## Objective Test–Form B

### Multiple Choice

In the blank after each item, write the letter of the best response. (5 points each, total 50)

1. Who is responsible for maintaining the integrity of an organization's records?      1. _____
   a. The librarian
   b. The administrative assistant
   c. The records clerk
   d. The records and information manager

2. Records and information management professionals often have a      2. _____
   a. master's degree in accounting, finance, or economics.
   b. Ph.D. in one of the business disciplines or in information and library science.
   c. two- or four-year degree in business or information and library science.
   d. bachelor's degree in liberal arts, computer science, or environmental engineering.

3. The records and information manager oversees the destruction of records when      3. _____
   a. the organization is unable to locate or afford additional storage space.
   b. they are no longer needed in the operations of the organization.
   c. they are no longer required for legal reasons.
   d. they are no longer needed in the operations of the organization or required for legal reasons.

4. Creation, distribution, maintenance, protection, control, storage, and destruction describe the      4. _____
   a. life cycle of records and information management.
   b. duties of the records clerk.
   c. functions of every business and organization.
   d. duties of the administrative assistant.

5. The records and information manager exercises records control within the organization by allowing access to records only to      5. _____
   a. the organization's employees.
   b. authorized persons.
   c. the records clerk.
   d. the administrative assistant.

6. A question that must be considered before a record is distributed is      6. _____
   a. How will the record be edited for accuracy?
   b. What medium will be used to create the record?
   c. How will the record be protected against disasters?
   d. How are copies to be sent to users?

**7.** An information system is a

    a. computer program for managing records.

    b. telephone system that can access records.

    c. way of planning, organizing, and developing information.

    d. set of books that describes how information is used.

7. _____

**8.** If the cost of creating a record

    a. exceeds its value to the business, then it probably should not be created.

    b. is less than its value to the business, then it probably should not be created.

    c. exceeds its value to the business, then it probably should be destroyed.

    d. is less than its value to the business, then it probably should be destroyed.

8. _____

**9.** If a record cannot be found,

    a. it is documented as being lost.

    b. it has no value to the organization.

    c. someone is assigned the job of reconstructing a similar record.

    d. someone is assigned the job of finding the record.

9. _____

**10.** The profession of records and information management consists of

    a. two groups: specialists in RIM and those whose occupation includes the management of information but who have another specialty or job title.

    b. two groups: specialists in RIM and computer programmers.

    c. three groups: specialists in RIM; computer programmers; and those whose occupation includes the management of information but who have another specialty or job title.

    d. two groups: those whose occupation includes the management of information but who have another specialty or job title, and computer programmers.

10. _____

## True or False

Circle T if the statement is true or F if the statement is false. (5 points each, total 50)

**11.** Maintaining the integrity of records means that they are kept in fireproof vaults at all times.     **11.** T  F

**12.** Records are stored and sometimes transferred to an inactive storage area once they are no longer in daily use.     **12.** T  F

**13.** Office managers, administrative assistants, engineers, and accountants should have a college major in RIM.     **13.** T  F

**14.** The activity of destruction is part of the function of records and information management.     **14.** T  F

**15.** Records should be protected from the hazards of fire and floods.     **15.** T  F

**16.** Records management deals with paper records, whereas information management deals with computer records.     **16.** T  F

**17.** The primary responsibility of the professional records and information manager is to store records when they become inactive.     **17.** T  F

**18.** Businesses do not have environmental protection policies because the government sets such policies.     **18.** T  F

**19.** Mail, fax machines, interoffice delivery, and electronic computer links are methods of distributing records to users.     **19.** T  F

**20.** *Filing* is the key word that should be considered in the storage function of RIM.     **20.** T  F

# CHAPTER 2
## Employment in Records and Information Management

## Objective Test—Form B

### Matching

In the blank after each definition, write the letter of the term that best matches the definition. Not all of the terms will be used. (4 points each, total 48)

**Terms**

|   |   |
|---|---|
| a. archival management | h. depository |
| b. archives | i. ICRM |
| c. archivist | j. government records management |
| d. ARMA International | k. legal records management |
| e. certified records manager | l. medical records management |
| f. consultant | m. records center |
| g. educational records management | n. SAA |

**Definitions**

1. certifying organization of professional records managers and administrative officers who specialize in the field of records and information management          1. _____

2. acronym for a group of institutional members who are concerned with the identification, preservation, and use of records of historical value          2. _____

3. a profession having to do with management of legal records          3. _____

4. the leading professional organization for persons in the expanding field of records and information management          4. _____

5. secure location, dedicated to the storage of all types of records that is usually part of the organization rather than a separate business          5. _____

6. job title for a person who maintains archives          6. _____

7. group of records, usually valuable and historical, that are not referred to on a daily basis for organizational operations          7. _____

8. maintaining a group of valuable records that are not referred to on a daily basis          8. _____

9. a professional designation granted by the ICRM          9. _____

10. secure location, dedicated to the storage of all types of documents and records that is usually a separate business          10. _____

11. person outside the organization who is hired to come into a business and make recommendations for more effective records systems          11. _____

12. a records management specialty that includes local, state, and federal records          12. _____

# True or False

Circle T if the statement is true or F if the statement is false. (4 points each, total 52)

13. The educational records management profession is often divided among local, state, and federal governments.                                       13. T  F

14. Hospitals, small manufacturers, and art retailers are examples of the types of organizations likely to employ archivists.                            14. T  F

15. A person who is responsible for ensuring the integrity of financial records has the duties of designing records systems, updating records, and designing controls.   15. T  F

16. The Institute of Certified Records Managers (ICRM) is the organization that oversees the professional designation of CRM.                            16. T  F

17. Employees in medical RIM may have a background in business, medical technology, medical records, nursing, insurance, or health care services.        17. T  F

18. Wills, deeds, birth certificates, marriage records, and tax records are several types of legal records that might be kept by a governmental unit such as a city or county.   18. T  F

19. The use of professional RIM consultants is decreasing.                       19. T  F

20. One of the benefits ARMA members receive from the organization is discounts on filing equipment.                                                     20. T  F

21. In addition to storing and protecting records, depositories and records centers might also film records, destroy records, and recover records after a disaster.   21. T  F

22. The financial records and information manager is more involved with the daily operations of business than the archivist.                             22. T  F

23. There are clearly defined categories of RIM specialties.                     23. T  F

24. One of the benefits of joining a professional organization is networking with other professionals to gather ideas and methods.                       24. T  F

25. Since the nature of records is changing as technology evolves, continued education for a records management professional is necessary.                25. T  F

# CHAPTER 3
## Legal and Ethical Matters in Records and Information Management

## Objective Test—Form B

### Matching
In the blank after each definition, write the letter of the term that best matches the definition. Not all of the terms will be used. (5 points each, total 25)

**Terms**
- a. admissibility into evidence
- b. civil law
- c. copyright
- d. criminal law
- e. litigation
- f. piracy

**Definitions**
1. to engage in a lawsuit                                                                          1. _____
2. an exclusive entitlement granted by the government for the publication of an artistic, musical, or written work       2. _____
3. to make illegal duplicates of copyrighted software                                              3. _____
4. statute covering a legal dispute between the government and an individual or business           4. _____
5. statute covering a legal dispute between one individual or business and another                 5. _____

### Multiple Choice
In the blank after each item, write the letter of the best response. (5 points each, total 25)

6. Admissibility into evidence refers to whether or not                                            6. _____
   a. a photocopy, microfilm copy, or computer software copy of a document will be accepted in court as valid evidence in a lawsuit.
   b. the organization is responsible for gathering, organizing, and presenting its documents as evidence in a lawsuit.
   c. the court is responsible for gathering, organizing, and presenting the organization's documents as evidence in a lawsuit.
   d. the organization is permitted to destroy its documents after they have been presented in a lawsuit.

7. An example of copyright infringement is                                                         7. _____
   a. records destruction.
   b. price fixing.
   c. a civil dispute.
   d. software piracy.

8. The source of information important to the government when determining whether or not a   8. _____
   business is abiding by laws and regulations dealing with business is
   a. archival records.
   b. all business records.
   c. active records.
   d. retention records.

9. Examples of ethical business management are   9. _____
   a. low pay and few benefits for employees, straightforward advertising, and manufacture of safe
      products.
   b. fair pay and benefits for employees, straightforward advertising, and price fixing.
   c. fair pay and benefits for employees, straightforward advertising, and honest pricing.
   d. fair pay and benefits for employees, deceptive advertising, and manufacturing of safe products.

10. The federal law that denies access to one's personal records without the individual's   10. _____
    permission is the
    a. Federal Reports Act.
    b. Federal Records Act.
    c. Freedom of Information Act.
    d. Privacy Act.

## True or False
Circle T if the statement is true or F if the statement is false. (5 points each, total 50)

11. Maintaining confidentiality of records is an example of how the RIM manager can observe   11. T  F
    high ethical standards.
12. Legal action by the government for noncompliance is a risk the RIM manager must be   12. T  F
    aware of.
13. Numerous local, state, and federal government laws and regulations have an impact upon   13. T  F
    how records and information are managed.
14. It is important for records and information managers to be familiar with criminal and civil   14. T  F
    laws and regulations.
15. The federal government allows state governments to determine whether or not citizens have   15. T  F
    the right to gain access to information about themselves.
16. Matters of business ethics have little relevance to the records and information management   16. T  F
    employee.
17. Bad morale is a likely result of straightforward advertising.   17. T  F
18. It is important that RIM employees refrain from destroying records that might be relevant to   18. T  F
    a lawsuit.
19. One may duplicate copyrighted items without permission of the owner if doing so for   19. T  F
    commercial use.
20. Good ethical business management by the RIM can result in increased employee loyalty and   20. T  F
    productivity.

# CHAPTER 4
## Receipt and Creation of Hard Copy Records

## Objective Test—Form B

### Matching

In the blank after each definition, write the letter of the term that best matches the definition. Not all of the terms will be used. (4 points each, total 40)

**Terms**

a. business forms          g. hard copy mail

b. discarded paperwork     h. incoming paperwork

c. e-mail                  i. internal paperwork

d. fax                     j. junk mail

e. form-filling software   k. outgoing paperwork

f. forms design software   l. voice mail

**Definitions**

1. paperwork arriving from and departing to offices inside the organization          1. _____

2. a recorded message transmitted from one telephone to another                      2. _____

3. computer software that helps in the design of efficient business forms            3. _____

4. a reproduction of a document sent from one machine to another over telephone lines  4. _____

5. paperwork arriving from others outside the organization                           5. _____

6. a means of sending a message or other document from one computer to one or more other computers  6. _____

7. computer programs that enable us to fill in business forms using the computer printer instead of a typewriter  7. _____

8. paperwork going to others outside the organization                                8. _____

9. paper records with blank spaces to be filled in and that must be carefully managed and designed  9. _____

10. any kind of mail that arrives on paper                                           10. _____

### Multiple Choice

In the blank after each item, write the letter of the best response. (4 points each, total 20)

11. To save paper when printing reports and other materials,                         11. _____
    a. include headers at the top of each page.
    b. use larger left, right, top, and bottom margins.
    c. single-space and print on both sides of the paper.
    d. use a laser printer.

12. Form-filling software is more efficient than filling out forms with a typewriter because it   12. _____
    a. allows a greater number of forms to be kept in storage.
    b. saves time by aligning copy to be filled in with the blank spaces on the form.
    c. saves time by allowing the user to enter the information that must appear on the paper form.
    d. allows the user to manipulate the design of the form.

13. To be classified as a record, a piece of paper must be   13. _____
    a. less costly to the organization when thrown away than when kept.
    b. equal in cost to the organization when thrown away and when kept.
    c. more costly to the organization when thrown away than when kept.
    d. kept temporarily or discarded immediately.

14. The first step in opening the mail in a small organization is to   14. _____
    a. prioritize.
    b. organize.
    c. classify.
    d. open.

15. Detailed instructions on a business form should appear   15. _____
    a. in the right margin.
    b. on the front.
    c. in the left margin.
    d. on the back.

## True or False
Circle T if the statement is true or F if the statement is false. (4 points each, total 40)

16. It is easy to figure the exact difference in the costs of keeping versus discarding paperwork.   16. T  F
17. Each incoming piece of paperwork is classified as a record to be kept.   17. T  F
18. Records and information managers are responsible for thinking carefully prior to allowing paperwork to be created.   18. T  F
19. Developments in technology have made it less tempting to produce paperwork.   19. T  F
20. The volume of paper received and the size of the organization determine how incoming paperwork is handled.   20. T  F
21. Large-volume copying jobs should be done on site, especially in small businesses.   21. T  F
22. Mail that comes in on paper is called hard copy mail.   22. T  F
23. It is important to keep track of who uses the copy machine and the number of copies made.   23. T  F
24. Create a record only if it serves the organization and its clients or customers.   24. T  F
25. When designing a business form, it is important to specify legal-size paper.   25. T  F

Name _____ Date _____ Score _____

Maximum Points: 100

# CHAPTER 5
## Indexing and Alphabetizing Procedures

## Objective Test—Form B

### Matching
In the blank after each definition, write the letter of the term that best matches the definition. Not all of the terms will be used. (3 points each, total 15)

**Terms**

    a. alphabetizing        d. lowercase

    b. case               e. units

    c. indexing          f. uppercase

**Definitions**

1. determining the order and format of the units in a name when alphabetizing      1. _____
2. small letters      2. _____
3. arranging in order according to the letters of the alphabet      3. _____
4. capital letters      4. _____
5. the name The Kozy Kiddie Korner, Inc., has five of these      5. _____

### Indexing
Write the *first indexing unit* of each name in the blank at the right. Omit any punctuation. The first item (0.) is an example. (2 points each, total 40)

    0. New York Insurance Co.    0. New
    6. 4 on the Floor Transmission Repair    6. _____
    7. Larry's Electronic Repairs    7. _____
    8. 9th Avenue Cameras    8. _____
    9. "Liz" for Show, Inc.    9. _____
    10. Sixty-Forty Trading Cards    10. _____
    11. Dr. Wool Fashions    11. _____
    12. 7-6 Day Care, Ltd.    12. _____
    13. Rev. Mary Claddock    13. _____
    14. The 98¢ Taco Hut    14. _____
    15. Pat O'Reilly    15. _____
    16. Police Dept., Wise, VA    16. _____
    17. Carlos de Hinesto    17. _____
    18. U.S. Dept. of State    18. _____
    19. The Roasty Toasty Grill    19. _____
    20. Wildlife Bureau, Canada    20. _____
    21. Monty Ellis-Kandies    21. _____
    22. R J Z Thrill Park    22. _____

**23.** Charlotte MacDonald      23._____

**24.** Roy Rogers Restaurant      24._____

**25.** Claude Eldon Slate      25._____

## Alphabetizing

In the blank at the right, indicate the alphabetic order of each name in the series of three names. The first item (0.) is an example. (3 points each, total 45)

  **0.** (a) Louis Pryor; (b) Lois Pryor; (c) M. Prime      **0.** cba

**26.** (a) 4th Street Bonding Co.; (b) 4 Your Wedding Accessories; (c) 40 Mile Beach Hotel      **26.** _____

**27.** (a) The O'Briens' Shop; (b) Sophia O'Brien; (c) Shirley O'Brian      **27.** _____

**28.** (a) Bud & Sam Candies; (b) Bud Answering Service; (c) The Bud and Rose Flower Shop      **28.** _____

**29.** (a) Kazan Bierominello; (b) Karen Beironnello; (c) Kastas Bieromnellio      **29.** _____

**30.** (a) 1-2-3 Computer College; (b) One for Your Money Hair Salon; (c) 1-Fine Time Travel Service      **30.** _____

**31.** (a) Alice Beckerman; (b) Bank of the Southwest; (c) Beck's Studios      **31.** _____

**32.** (a) Merino's Check Cashing Service; (b) Cora Marino; (c) Consuelo Meriam, Jr.      **32.** _____

**33.** (a) The Carriage House; (b) Carriage of Contentment, Inc.; (c) Carriage by Nicholas, Ltd.      **33.** _____

**34.** (a) Wm. Scully; (b) Willard Scolly; (c) W. O. Scully-Weston      **34.** _____

**35.** (a) U.S. Dept. of Justice; (b) United States Gypsum Co.; (c) United Stay-Fast Co.      **35.** _____

**36.** (a) Chas. Wilt Co.; (b) Cecil Wilson; (c) Charley Wilt, Inc.      **36.** _____

**37.** (a) Dalton Co., 226 Moyer Ave., Oakland, CA; (b) Dalton Co., Massey Dr., Oxnard, CA; (c) Dalton Co., 12472 Moyer Ave., Oakland, CA      **37.** _____

**38.** (a) West-Berry, Inc.; (b) Western Laundromat; (c) West and Brill, Inc.      **38.** _____

**39.** (a) Public Schools, City of Alberta; (b) Alberta Door Mfg. Co.; (c) Alberta Classroom Supplies      **39.** _____

**40.** (a) W. Allen Brown; (b) Brown-Young Pharmacists; (c) Bryan Brown      **40.** _____

# CHAPTER 6
## Systems for Organizing Paper Records

# Objective Test—Form B

## Matching

In the blank after each definition, write the letter of the term that best matches the definition. Not all of the terms will be used. (3 points each, total 60)

### Terms

a. ADA
b. alphabetic
c. chronological
d. cross-reference
e. cut
f. dictionary
g. ELF
h. encyclopedic

i. ergonomics
j. file folder
k. file guide
l. file label
m. filing equipment
n. filing supplies
o. geographic
p. indirect

q. numeric
r. subject
s. subject-numeric
t. system entry
u. system storage
v. tab

### Definitions

1. arrangement of files in alphabetic order by subject captions with no subheadings          1. _____
2. small adhesive tag used to identify folders and guides          2. _____
3. cardboard divider used to support folders and identify file sections          3. _____
4. system for organizing records by date          4. _____
5. system for organizing records by topic          5. _____
6. similar to encyclopedic subject systems except that numbers are used to identify the captions          6. _____
7. system for organizing records according to the sequence of letters in the alphabet          7. _____
8. a campaign by ARMA to eliminate legal-size files and legal-size paper          8. _____
9. file folders and pockets for paper records and accessories such as file dividers and labels          9. _____
10. the width of a folder or guide tab relative to the width of the folder or guide          10. _____
11. system for organizing records according to preassigned or assigned numbers          11. _____
12. any filing system that requires reference to an index before the records can be located          12. _____
13. legislation that includes requirements for accessibility to equipment by persons who have disabilities          13. _____
14. alphabetic arrangement of records by subject captions with headings and subheadings          14. _____
15. consists primarily of file containers and cabinets and filing accessories          15. _____
16. system for organizing records by locality, area, or territory          16. _____
17. the applied science of conforming equipment, systems, and the working environment to the requirements of people, including those who have disabilities          17. _____
18. a heavy paper container for filed records          18. _____
19. a notation that a record is filed in another location          19. _____
20. an extension at the top of a folder or guide where a label is placed for identification          20. _____

## Multiple Choice

In the blank after each item, write the letter of the best response. (4 points each, total 20)

21. The best candidates for subject filing are
    a. numbered forms such as invoices, requisitions, and checks.
    b. employee records such as applications for employment and pay records.
    c. records that refer to products, processes, and formulas.
    d. records that refer to locality, area, or sales territory.

    21. _____

22. Records should be stored inside a file folder with the front facing the user and the heading to the
    a. right.
    b. left.
    c. top.
    d. bottom.

    22. _____

23. ADA stands for
    a. Americans with Disabilities Act.
    b. American Disabilities Association.
    c. American Database Association.
    d. Association for Directors of America.

    23. _____

24. The purpose of a file guide is to
    a. contain significant correspondence arranged in order by number.
    b. support file folders and to label major sections of the file.
    c. identify the location, area, or territory of the file equipment.
    d. contain significant correspondence arranged in order by date.

    24. _____

25. A letter book contains correspondence in order by
    a. subject and number.
    b. subject.
    c. number.
    d. date.

    25. _____

## True or False

Circle T if the statement is true or F if the statement is false. (2 points each, total 20)

26. Lawyers, physicians, and dentists will most likely arrange their client and patient folders in order by subject.

    26. T  F

27. Labels for folders and guides can be printed from a computer database or keyed on a typewriter.

    27. T  F

28. Additional floor space is one example of an extra cost associated with using paper records systems.

    28. T  F

29. The storage documentation step is mandatory for both large-scale and small-scale systems.

    29. T  F

30. Legal-size files and paper are more costly than standard-size equipment and paper.

    30. T  F

31. Subject-numeric files are similar to dictionary subject files except numbers are used to identify the captions.   **31.** T  F

32. Ergonomic factors include geographic, subject, and numeric filing of records.   **32.** T  F

33. Numeric filing is a direct system.   **33.** T  F

34. Motorized files are less expensive to purchase and repair than are manually operated equipment.   **34.** T  F

35. A sales business with definite geographic sales areas would be likely to organize certain records geographically by sales territory.   **35.** T  F

# CHAPTER 7
## Retrieval, Retention, and Recycling

## Objective Test—Form B

### Matching

In the blank after each definition, write the letter of the term that best matches the definition. Not all of the terms will be used. (5 points each, total 50)

**Terms**

a. by-product information
b. disintegrator
c. electronic access
d. incinerate
e. network
f. out guide

g. pulping
h. recovery
i. recycle
j. requisition
k. retention
l. retention schedule

**Definitions**

1. to destroy records by burning them                                                          1. _____
2. a written request for records                                                                    2. _____
3. a process used to destroy records by adding water and creating a slurry mixture   3. _____
4. a group of facts created for a secondary reason                                          4. _____
5. the period of time records are kept, or retained                                          5. _____
6. a heavy paper signpost that documents the location from which a record was removed, the name of the record, the borrower, and the date                                         6. _____
7. form that lists each type of record and the number of years each is to be retained   7. _____
8. to manufacture paper and other products from waste, scrap, used paper, and other items   8. _____
9. a group of computers linked electronically                                                9. _____
10. a machine that chops materials into small pieces                                       10. _____

### True or False

Circle T if the statement is true or F if the statement is false. (5 points each, total 50)

11. The primary purpose of the documentation component of retrieval is to make a record of where documents are filed.                                    **11.** T   F

12. Follow-up is the component of retrieval in which records employees communicate with users if borrowed records are due.                             **12.** T   F

13. In the delivery component of retrieval, records are delivered to a records storage area to be filed.                                                **13.** T   F

14. Records retention is probably the most complex and difficult issue that the professional records and information manager must address.                **14.** T   F

15. Electronic access to records has become the norm in recent years.      **15.** T   F

16. Federal, state, and local governments allow organizations to use their own discretion when deciding whether to keep or destroy records.               **16.** T   F

17. Cost is one of the five major components in the retrieval function.       **17.** T  F

18. Three major considerations in destroying records are cost, security, and environmental protection.       **18.** T  F

19. The three Rs of records and information management are retrieval, retention, and recycling.       **19.** T  F

20. A precise retention schedule can be one result of a well-planned retention policy.       **20.** T  F

# CHAPTER 8
## Managing Electronic Files

## Objective Test—Form B

### True or False
Circle T if the statement is true or F if the statement is false. (2 points each, total 20)

1. A folder can contain files but not other folders.                                              **1.** T F
2. Tapes and CD-R discs can be used to create file system backups.                                **2.** T F
3. The file type should not be changed.                                                           **3.** T F
4. The subject of a Microsoft Office document is part of the metadata.                            **4.** T F
5. The D drive is typically a hard drive.                                                         **5.** T F
6. The operating system is used to manage your appointments.                                      **6.** T F
7. A missing file can always be retrieved from the last incremental backup tape.                  **7.** T F
8. Folder names in Windows 95 can have only twenty characters.                                    **8.** T F
9. *Find* can locate files based on text known to exist in the document.                          **9.** T F
10. When sending an electronic document to a customer, the file name should include the           **10.** T F
    document tracking number.

### Matching
In the blank after each definition, write the letter of the term that best matches the definition. Not all of the terms will be used. (2 points each, total 20)

**Terms**

| | |
|---|---|
| a. application | g. file system |
| b. association | h. hardware |
| c. byte | i. metadata |
| d. CPU | j. operating system |
| e. digital | k. shortcut |
| f. file | l. storage device |

**Definitions**

11. a file that contains instructions for creating or manipulating electronic records        **11.** _____
12. the brain of the computer                                                                 **12.** _____
13. the computer's hard drive is an example                                                   **13.** _____
14. computers that manipulate numbers                                                         **14.** _____
15. a program that manages the computer's hardware and acts as a manager of other programs    **15.** _____
16. a set of folders and files set up as a hierarchical means of storing electronic records on the   **16.** _____
    computer
17. the physical parts of a computer, such as the CPU and monitor                             **17.** _____
18. a special file used only for telling the operating system the location of another file    **18.** _____
19. where a single character on a computer is stored                                          **19.** _____
20. information about the contents of a file                                                  **20.** _____

# Multiple Choice

In the blank after each item, write the letter of the best response. (3 points each, total 30)

21. In the file called *MyFile.txt*, the characters *txt* are the
    a. filetype.
    b. association.
    c. abbreviation.
    d. file name.

    21. _____

22. The following are storage devices except
    a. the floppy disk.
    b. the CD-ROM.
    c. the CPU.
    d. tape.

    22. _____

23. An electronic file drawer that is accessed directly using a drive letter is called the
    a. top folder.
    b. main folder.
    c. prime directory.
    d. root directory.

    23. _____

24. The following are examples of metadata except
    a. the creation date.
    b. keywords.
    c. the C: drive.
    d. the file size.

    24. _____

25. A file name called *JohnHarrison is a \*.doc* is not a legal file name in MS Windows because it
    a. has too many characters.
    b. contains spaces.
    c. contains a *.
    d. does not use numbers.

    25. _____

26. The following principles should be followed when naming files except
    a. identification.
    b. grammatical correctness.
    c. brevity.
    d. documentation.

    26. _____

27. The set of requirements that make up a search for electronic records is called
    a. the search pattern.
    b. search rules.
    c. criteria.
    d. the methodology.

    27. _____

**28.** The electronic equivalent of a file drawer that contains multiple documents is a

    a. multi-store.

    b. directory.

    c. shortcut.

    d. filing space.

28. _____

**29.** A backup that includes only files that changed since the last backup is called a(n)

    a. incomplete backup.

    b. change backup.

    c. full backup.

    d. incremental backup.

29. _____

**30.** The one program required for the computer to function is the

    a. CPU.

    b. word processor.

    c. calculator program.

    d. operating system.

30. _____

## Short Answer

In the blank after each definition, write the term that best matches the definition. (3 points each, total 30)

**31.** When printing electronic documents, you should include the _____ as part of the header or footer so that others can find the electronic version.

31. _____

**32.** The monitor, printer, and speakers are all called _____.

32. _____

**33.** The part of a document name that allows the operating system to associate a program is called the _____.

33. _____

**34.** Multiple filing methodologies can be implemented with the same electronic records by using _____.

34. _____

**35.** The *A* drive in a Windows computer must be a(n) _____ drive.

35. _____

**36.** The advanced search feature of Microsoft Office allows the user to find files based on specific _____.

36. _____

**37.** An outside recipient can verify the source of an electronic document if you include a(n) _____.

37. _____

**38.** The MS Windows operating systems provide a file search tool called _____.

38. _____

**39.** The set of electronic instructions that computers use to create and manipulate other electronic documents is called a(n) _____.

39. _____

**40.** In a digital computer, the character z is represented with a(n) _____.

40. _____

# CHAPTER 9
## Using Electronic Databases

## Objective Test—Form B

### Multiple Choice I
In the blank after each item, write the letter of the best response. (3 points each, total 15)

1. A field used to store only a limited number of known values is usually created as a       1. _____
   a. short string.
   b. limited string.
   c. list.
   d. number.

2. A table is created to hold the names and addresses of all customers. A second table is       2. _____
   created to hold all product orders. The two tables are then connected using a
   a. link.
   b. shortcut.
   c. tether.
   d. relation.

3. In the example in question 2, people can view the connected tables because records in each       3. _____
   of the tables have a special field containing identical values. This field is called a(n)
   a. tag.
   b. key.
   c. ID.
   d. connector.

4. The process of deciding how to divide fields into related tables and thus remove duplication       4. _____
   is called
   a. bisecting.
   b. relating.
   c. linking.
   d. normalization.

5. In a query, the rules that determine which information is displayed are called       5. _____
   a. query rules.
   b. questions.
   c. criteria.
   d. requests.

# Matching I

In the blank after each definition, write the letter of the term that best matches the definition. Not all of the terms will be used. (2 points each, total 20)

**Terms**

a. dbms                    h. object
b. field                   i. query
c. form                    j. rdbms
d. key                     k. record
e. memo                    l. report
f. normalization           m. string
g. numeric                 n. table

**Definitions**

6. the structure that stores data for multiple entries                                                    6. _____

7. a question that you ask the database                                                                   7. _____

8. a field that should be used for storage whenever mathematical calculations are used on data            8. _____

9. the process of splitting information into multiple related tables in such a way that pieces of         9. _____
   data are not repeated

10. where a single piece of information (like a phone number) is stored                                   10. _____

11. where multiple pieces of information, related to a single item or activity, are stored                11. _____

12. pictures, files, and other large pieces of data are stored as this in the database                    12. _____

13. because of particular sorting requirements, it is best to store a zip code as this                     13. _____

14. a piece of information that is considered unique and is used to identify an item or activity           14. _____

15. often used for entry and one-record-at-a-time viewing of database information                          15. _____

# True or False

Circle T if the statement is true or F if the statement is false. (2 points each, total 20)

16. Information can be stored only in tables.                                                              16. T F

17. Records are stored in a table in alphabetical order.                                                  17. T  F

18. A key field in two or more tables is used to create a relation.                                       18. T  F

19. A field can store a string and a number simultaneously.                                               19. T  F

20. A list is used when a field can have only a few specific values.                                      20. T  F

21. Forms exist only to help the user enter and view information in the database.                          21. T  F

22. Normalization usually increases the amount of information in the database.                             22. T  F

23. Queries are the primary means of entering information into the database.                               23. T  F

24. Pictures, videos, and other nonstandard information can be stored in a database as an                  24. T  F
    object.

25. Searching for documents on the Web can be accomplished only using mathematical                         25. T  F
    equations.

# Matching II

In the blank after each field definition, write the letter of the field type that is most appropriate for the information to be stored. (2 points each, total 30)

**Field Types**

    a. date                   e. memo

    b. link                   f. number

    c. list                   g. object

    d. logical             h. string

**Field Name: Description**

Questions 26–33 are fields in a hospital's patient database.

26. Bloodtype: A, B, AB, or O                 26. _____

27. MaritalStatus: Single, Married, Divorced, Widowed, or Separated   27. _____

28. Birthdate: the month/day/year of birth           28. _____

29. TimeIn: the time of day the patient was checked in     29. _____

30. Total Cost: sum of the room charge, medicine charge, labor, and taxes   30. _____

31. Symptoms: description of symptoms as relayed by the patient (should handle three paragraphs)   31. _____

32. Insurer: name of the insurance company         32. _____

33. RHFactor: + or −                  33. _____

Questions 34–40 are fields in an online bookseller's database.

34. Review: location of file containing book review     34. _____

35. BookTitle: the formal title of the book         35. _____

36. ISBN: the book's identification number in the Library of Congress (must look like 1-55812-306-9)   36. _____

37. BookCover: an image of the book cover         37. _____

38. Genre: one of a predefined set of strings such as Mystery or Comedy   38. _____

39. Hardback: true if the book is a hardback        39. _____

40. CustomerID: used as the customer table key field    40. _____

# Multiple Choice II

In the blank after each item, write the letter of the string size that is most appropriate for the field. The majority of entries will fit with a minimum waste of space. (3 points each, total 15)

                                   41. _____

41. Month of the year (e.g., January)

    a. 4

    b. 3

    c. 9

    d. 12

                                     42. _____

42. A zip code (e.g., 11234-5679)

    a. 30

    b. 10

    c. 5

    d. 9

**43.** Personal title (e.g., Mr., Ms., etc.)

    a. 1

    b. 2

    c. 4

    d. 10

**43.** _____

**44.** Street name (e.g., First St.)

    a. 5

    b. 10

    c. 25

    d. 100

**44.** _____

**45.** United States Postal Service abbreviations for U.S. states

    a. 2

    b. 6

    c. 25

    d. 13

**45.** _____

# CHAPTER 10
## Network-Based Records Management

## Objective Test—Form B

### True or False
Circle T if the statement is true or F if the statement is false. (2 points each, total 20)

1. A Web browser is software that acts as a client on the network.                    1. T  F
2. A shared folder can be accessed by anyone on the Internet.                          2. T  F
3. A TLD can be an organizational designation or a country code.                        3. T  F
4. A file server requests files from other computers.                                   4. T  F
5. A person with *read* access to a network document cannot modify it.                 5. T  F
6. A folder's share name must be the same as its computer name.                        6. T  F
7. Network equipment is used to ensure that a message gets from one computer to another.  7. T  F
8. Hyperlinks increase the speed of your LAN cables.                                     8. T  F
9. Computers on a network must all have a unique address.                               9. T  F
10. Searching for documents on the Web can be accomplished only using mathematical     10. T  F
    equations.

### Multiple Choice
In the blank after each item, write the letter of the best response. (3 points each, total 30)

11. In a computer network, a protocol is                                               11. _____
    a. a special piece of computer hardware for accessing the network.
    b. what is used when you write your e-mail message to the boss.
    c. a new technology for downloading Web pages quickly.
    d. a set of rules and codes that allow computers to communicate with each other.

12. The following are all network equipment except the                                 12. _____
    a. hub.
    b. router.
    c. switch.
    d. scanner.

13. The domain name wlu.edu is the Internet site for a                                 13. _____
    a. high school.
    b. college or university.
    c. large electronics company.
    d. vocational learning center.

**14.** All computers that operate on a network must have a(n)
    a. server license.
    b. e-mail account.
    c. address.
    d. monitor.

14. _____

**15.** All of the following are valid file permissions except
    a. read.
    b. change.
    c. authorize.
    d. none of the above.

15. _____

**16.** A computer using Windows 3.1 would see a shared file name called *JohnHarrison.letter.doc* as
    a. $JOHN1%@sdf@#$
    b. JohnHarr.letter
    c. JohnHarrison.letter.doc
    d. JOHNHA ~ 1.DOC

16. _____

**17.** *Larrysmith@majorcorp.com* is a(n)
    a. Web page.
    b. small computer at the MajorCorp company.
    c. e-mail address.
    d. shortcut to a shared folder.

17. _____

**18.** The following designations are all top-level domains except
    a. com
    b. edu
    c. dell
    d. us

18. _____

**19.** A shared folder can be accessed by
    a. computers anywhere on the Internet.
    b. people with a valid e-mail address.
    c. computers using the same LAN.
    d. Web servers.

19. _____

**20.** A domain name allows computers on the Internet
    a. to secure their documents.
    b. to be uniquely identified.
    c. to violate network protocols.
    d. to control other computers.

20. _____

## Short Answer I

In the blank after each definition, write the term that best matches the definition. (3 points each, total 15)

21. A person who can view a file in a shared folder but not make changes to it has _____ access to that folder.

21. _____

22. One of the methods of accessing shared folders and drives from a remote location is _____.

22. _____

23. In the URL *http://www.abc.com/top/sales/kentucky/oct.html*, the relative path of the document is _____.

23. _____

24. The set of electronic codes that allow computers to communicate with each other on a network is called _____.

24. _____

25. Access to a file server can be made in an MS Windows environment using the Network Neighborhood, or by making it appear that another disk is available by creating a(n) _____.

25. _____

## Matching

In the blank after each definition, write the letter of the term that best matches the definition. Not all of the terms will be used. (2 points each, total 20)

### Terms

a. domain name
b. e-mail
c. ethernet
d. Internet
e. LAN
f. modem
g. path
h. peer
i. protocol
j. server
k. shared
l. top-level domain

### Definitions

26. a set of electronic codes that computers on the network all understand and that allows them to start a communication

26. _____

27. a computer that both requests information from and provides information to another computer

27. _____

28. a type of cable used as network media, to carry electronic information from computer to computer

28. _____

29. a folder on your computer that allows other computers on the network to access it

29. _____

30. the network media, protocols, and equipment located within a single office or business

30. _____

31. the name of a computer used as a Web address on the Internet (e.g., *www.companyname.com*)

31. _____

32. a message sent from one person to another across a network

32. _____

33. the part of an Internet document address that includes the computer, folders, and file name

33. _____

34. a network of networks that connects many LANs together so that messages and documents can be sent from one network to another

34. _____

35. a computer whose job is to wait for a request for an electronic document and send it to the requesting computer

35. _____

## Short Answer II

In the blank after each definition, write the letter of the term that best matches the definition. (3 points each, total 15)

36. The wires or fiber-optic cable or radio waves that carry information on a network are called _____.

36. _____

37. In the URL *http://www.abc.com/top/sales/kentucky/oct.html*, the characters *www.abc.com* are called the _____.

37. _____

38. A computer (or program) that usually requests information from other computers (or programs) on a network is called a(n) _____.

38. _____

39. The U.S. Senate, IRS, National Institutes of Health, and NASA all have a top-level domain (TLD) of _____.

39. _____

40. In the URL *http://www.abc.com/top/sales/kentucky/oct.html*, the characters *http:* are called the _____.

40. _____

# CHAPTER 11
## Image Technology and Automated Systems

## Objective Test—Form B

### Matching I

In the blank after each definition, write the letter of the term that best matches the definition. Not all of the terms will be used. (2 points each, total 30)

**Terms**

a. bar code      i. microfiche

b. CD-R      j. microfilm

c. CD-RW      k. microfilmer

d. data image      l. microform or microrecord

e. disk technology      m. optical character recognition

f. DVD      n. reader or viewer

g. image scanner      o. real image

h. image technology      p. redundancy

**Definitions**

1. pattern of bars, or lines, that have a unique meaning and represent a single document or file      1. _____

2. a camera specially designed to take pictures of documents onto microfilm or microfiche      2. _____

3. information, rather than a picture, captured from paper and converted to electronic form      3. _____

4. a flat, transparent film sheet containing microforms      4. _____

5. a machine into which paper documents are fed for conversion to electronic form, usually onto one of several types of disks      5. _____

6. an exact reproduction on film or in electronic form of a paper record      6. _____

7. the use of computer disks to store real images      7. _____

8. digital video disk; an emerging technology that may replace conventional compact disk technology      8. _____

9. compact disk-recordable; a relatively inexpensive compact disk onto which data can be recorded once      9. _____

10. the conversion of paper records to photographic or electronic form and the administration of the new form      10. _____

11. a machine that magnifies the miniature images of a microform and displays them on a screen      11. _____

12. compact disk-rewritable; a compact disk onto which new data can be recorded over old data      12. _____

13. duplication      13. _____

14. a miniature picture of a single paper record on a microfilm roll or microfiche      14. _____

15. a 16-mm, 35-mm, or 105-mm roll of film containing microforms      15. _____

# True or False

Circle T if the statement is true or F if the statement is false. (2 points each, total 30)

16. When selecting an automated records management system, architecture should be decided on before other factors are considered.  **16.** T  F

17. Three major considerations in choosing an automated records management system are functions, cost, and architecture.  **17.** T  F

18. MICR technology is used primarily in the insurance industry.  **18.** T  F

19. Both conventional and imaging (full-text) automated records management systems require computer software.  **19.** T  F

20. Automated records management systems are software programs that make files, documents, and other records accessible for management by computer.  **20.** T  F

21. Although the initial installation of a bar coding system is expensive, it can pay for itself within as little as one year.  **21.** T  F

22. The U.S. Postal Service has yet to adopt bar-coding technology.  **22.** T  F

23. Bar codes are read by scanners.  **23.** T  F

24. With CD-R disks, you can erase but not record information.  **24.** T  F

25. DVD technology is gradually being phased out.  **25.** T  F

26. In the term RAID, the letters RA mean "read access."  **26.** T  F

27. Image scanning technology is newer than micrographic technology.  **27.** T  F

28. Micrographic technology greatly reduces the cost of storage space.  **28.** T  F

29. CD-RW and CD-R are both inexpensive disks.  **29.** T  F

30. Both microfilm and microfiche are microrecords.  **30.** T  F

# Matching II

In the blank after each definition, write the letter of the term that best matches the definition. Not all of the terms will be used. (2 points each, total 30)

## Terms

a. architecture
b. background processes
c. batch processes
d. Boolean logic search
e. charge back
f. charge-out and return
g. command-driven
h. conventional
i. global modification

j. GUI
k. icon
l. keyword search
m. menu-driven
n. phrase search
o. reservation
p. toggle
q. waiting list
r. wild card search

## Definitions

31. screen picture selected by a mouse to operate a system that is menu-driven  **31.** _____

32. characteristics of hardware and software used in an automated system  **32.** _____

33. to document the loan of an item and note its return  **33.** _____

34. system operation method in which the user must enter keywords or instructions  **34.** _____

35. feature that enables the user to select screen options and operate the system with a keyboard, a mouse, or other input device, and uses graphic images, windows, forms, and icons  **35.** _____

36. a system feature in which a group of records can be processed all at one time  **36.** _____

37. using two or more consecutive words in a field to find a record  **37.** _____

**38.** a systems feature that permits processes such as queries and indexing to be executed while the user performs other functions within the program  38. _____

**39.** using any single word in a field to find a record  39. _____

**40.** addition or deletion made throughout a system with a single command  40. _____

**41.** to use a symbol, such as * or ?, to look for records when some of the information is missing  41. _____

**42.** query using more than one keyword or phrase and a logic statement (*AND, OR, NOT, EXCEPT, IF, THEN*) to limit or expand the scope of the search  42. _____

**43.** request-handling feature that enables an item to be held for delivery on a specified date  43. _____

**44.** feature that places a potential user on a list for records that have been charged out  44. _____

**45.** feature that enables the user to switch between one program and another without exiting either  45. _____

# Multiple Choice

In the blank after each item, write the letter of the best response. (2 points each, total 10)

**46.** Factors considered in the architecture of an automated records management system include the  46. _____
   a. quality of the software being purchased.
   b. management functions that the system will perform.
   c. total cost of the automated system.
   d. types of computers on which the software will run.

**47.** Container management refers to  47. _____
   a. controlling active and inactive records in a central location.
   b. containing costs in the operation of automated records management systems.
   c. delivering records to users in approved file boxes and other containers.
   d. reserving space for and monitoring the contents of file containers.

**48.** Major functions of automated records management systems include all of the following except management of  48. _____
   a. records center employees.
   b. all types of active records.
   c. records for a specific industry.
   d. records retention.

**49.** Total costs for an automated records management system consist of  49. _____
   a. overhead, such as costs of heat and electricity.
   b. initial outlay, maintenance, support, and training.
   c. the amount paid for the system software and hardware.
   d. salaries of those operating the system.

**50.** Menu-driven systems  50. _____
   a. require entry of keywords or instructions.
   b. are used primarily in the restaurant industry.
   c. permit the user to select from a list of choices.
   d. require a menu driver to boot the system.

Name _____ Date _____ Score _____

# CHAPTER 12
## Safety, Security, and Disaster Recovery

## Objective Test–Form B

### Matching I

In the blank after each definition, write the letter of the term that best matches the definition. Not all of the terms will be used. (3 points each, total 30)

**Terms**

a. authentication
b. battery backup
c. carpal tunnel syndrome
d. electronic vaulting
e. facial recognition
f. fingerprint scanner
g. human disaster

h. integrated security system
i. natural disaster
j. password
k. smart card
l. sprinkler system
m. surge protector
n. voice-input computer

**Definitions**

1. service of storing backup copies of vital electronic records          1. _____
2. the identification code used as part of an authentication system       2. _____
3. a unit between the computer power cord and the electrical outlet that can calm electrical current overloads and thus prevent the destruction of data          3. _____
4. computer and software that enable the user to speak into a microphone to enter data into a computer system          4. _____
5. small microprocessor used for access to a storage area          5. _____
6. series of devices that spray water automatically when excess heat is sensed          6. _____
7. methods of controlling access to facilities such as office buildings, floors, and rooms          7. _____
8. system that provides standby power to a computer system in case of a temporary loss of electrical power          8. _____
9. an injury to the wrist that can be caused by the repetitive motions of working at a computer keyboard          9. _____
10. type of biometric access control device that reads the characteristics of a person's face          10. _____

### True or False

Circle T if the statement is true or F if the statement is false. (2 points each, total 20)

11. Paper documents exposed to water damage can often be restored by using one of the drying techniques.          11. T  F
12. The RIM should consider the costs prior to the selection of a records security system.          12. T  F
13. When recovering wet paper, take immediate action to avoid the accumulation of mold.          13. T  F
14. A records manager cannot prevent human disasters from happening.          14. T  F

15. The use of an ergonomic keyboard should be considered as one way to reduce repetitive motion injuries.  **15.** T  F

16. A nuclear accident is a human disaster.  **16.** T  F

17. Equipment and buildings have improved, resulting in disaster preparedness becoming somewhat less important in recent years.  **17.** T  F

18. Companies use a firewall to scramble and unscramble data being sent over the Internet.  **18.** T  F

19. Unlike paper records, records stored in electronic databases are free from possible destruction.  **19.** T  F

20. Many records can be saved after being exposed to the heat, smoke, and flames of a serious fire.  **20.** T  F

## Multiple Choice

In the blank after each item, write the letter of the best response. (4 points each, total 20)

21. Records security measures protect records from different types of risks such as  **21.** _____
    a. improper access, accidental loss, theft, damage, and unwanted destruction.
    b. misplacing the records and not organizing the records in proper order within file drawers.
    c. electrical circuit overload, file tipping, and collisions.
    d. carpal tunnel syndrome, electrical circuit overload, and misplacing records within file drawers.

22. The first step in avoiding injuries in records areas is to  **22.** _____
    a. avoid overloading electrical circuits.
    b. avoid tripping over electrical cords on walkways.
    c. speak to the records workers about safety precautions.
    d. develop a written, comprehensive safety plan.

23. The purpose of an authentication system is to  **23.** _____
    a. avoid the misplacement of paper records and computer data.
    b. protect the data in a computer or computer network by controlling user access.
    c. protect and control access to facilities such as office buildings, floors, and rooms.
    d. prevent paper record damage by converting printed text and graphics to computer data.

24. Biometric access control devices can evaluate physical characteristics of a person's  **24.** _____
    a. weight.
    b. heartbeat.
    c. eyes.
    d. height.

25. According to Chapter 12, UPS stands for  **25.** _____
    a. United Parcel Service.
    b. uninterruptible power source.
    c. uninterruptible password system.
    d. unidentified password security.

# Matching II

In the blank after each definition, write the letter of the term that best matches the definition. Not all of the terms will be used. (3 points each, total 30)

## Terms

a. air drying
b. black box
c. computer virus
d. detector
e. disaster recovery
f. electronic key

g. electronic security card
h. freeze drying
i. repetitive motion injury
j. scanner
k. UPS
l. voice-activated

## Definitions

**26.** unwanted program instructions that can alter and destroy data                     26. _____

**27.** electronic access control plastic passkey without the grooves of traditional keys   27. _____

**28.** biometric access control system that reads voice patterns                          28. _____

**29.** technology that uses a communication security device containing information about    29. _____
authorized users

**30.** damage to nerves and muscles caused by repetitive movement                         30. _____

**31.** executing plans for saving as many records as possible after a disaster            31. _____

**32.** electronic control access device that looks like a credit card, with a magnetic strip on   32. _____
one side

**33.** input device that converts printed text and graphics to computer data             33. _____

**34.** technique for removing water from soaked records by first freezing them and then allowing   34. _____
the ice to melt and evaporate

**35.** technique for removing water from soaked documents by placing them on polyester    35. _____
webbing and allowing the water to evaporate

# COMPREHENSIVE TESTS, FORMS A AND B

# COMPREHENSIVE TEST—FORM A
## Chapters 1–12

## Multiple Choice
In the blank after each item, write the letter of the best response. (1 point each, total 40)

1. In a database query, the rules that determine what information is displayed are called
   a. query rules.
   b. questions.
   c. criteria.
   d. requests.

   1. _____

2. A database table is created to hold the names and addresses of all customers. A second table is created to hold all product orders. The two tables are then connected using a
   a. link.
   b. shortcut.
   c. relation.
   d. tether.

   2. _____

3. Creation, distribution, maintenance, protection, control, storage, and destruction describe the
   a. life cycle of records and information management.
   b. duties of the records clerk.
   c. functions of every business and organization.
   d. duties of the administrative assistant.

   3. _____

4. The first step in opening the mail in a small organization is to
   a. prioritize.
   b. organize.
   c. classify.
   d. open.

   4. _____

5. To save paper when printing reports and other materials,
   a. include headers at the top of each page.
   b. use larger left, right, top, and bottom margins.
   c. single-space and print on both sides of the paper.
   d. use a laser printer.

   5. _____

**6.** Detailed instructions on a business form should appear      6. _____

    a. in the right margin.

    b. on the front.

    c. in the left margin.

    d. on the back.

**7.** The following principles should be followed in naming electronic files except      7. _____

    a. identification.

    b. grammatical correctness.

    c. brevity.

    d. documentation.

**8.** To be classified as a record, a piece of paper must be      8. _____

    a. less costly to the organization when thrown away than when kept.

    b. equal in cost to the organization when thrown away and when kept.

    c. more costly to the organization when thrown away than when kept.

    d. kept temporarily or discarded immediately.

**9.** The best file name for a letter written on May 4 to Kennitt Company is      9. _____

    a. Letter

    b. 5_4Letter Kennitt

    c. Kennitt Letter May 4

    d. Kenlet

**10.** The file name abbreviation that, when pronounced, sounds most like Hannsborough is      10. _____

    a. Hannsbor.

    b. Hansboro.

    c. Hnnbough.

    d. Hborough.

**11.** In a file name, July 8 would best be represented in three characters as      11. _____

    a. J08

    b. JU8

    c. 8JY

    d. 708

**12.** An electronic folder that is accessed directly, without the need to access any other folders, is a      12. _____

    a. directory folder.

    b. root folder.

    c. file folder.

    d. window folder.

**13.** *Larrysmith@majorcorp.com* is a(n)      13. _____

    a. e-mail address.

    b. Web page.

    c. small computer at Major Corporation.

    d. shortcut to a shared folder.

**14.** The procedure of regularly copying the contents of computers onto another medium is called making a(n)
    a. alias.
    b. backup.
    c. attachment.
    d. hyperlink.

14. _____

**15.** Major functions of automated records management systems include all of the following except management of
    a. records center employees.
    b. all types of active records.
    c. records for a specific industry.
    d. records retention.

15. _____

**16.** The first step in avoiding injuries in records areas is to
    a. avoid overloading electrical circuits.
    b. avoid tripping over electrical cords on walkways.
    c. speak to the records workers about safety precautions.
    d. develop a written, comprehensive safety plan.

16. _____

**17.** The purpose of a file guide is to
    a. contain significant correspondence arranged in order by number.
    b. support file folders and to label major sections of the file.
    c. identify the location, area, or territory of the file equipment.
    d. contain significant correspondence arranged in order by date.

17. _____

**18.** Information about information is known as
    a. software.
    b. hardware.
    c. metadata.
    d. criteria.

18. _____

**19.** Records security measures protect records from different types of risks such as
    a. improper access, accidental loss, theft, damage, and unwanted destruction.
    b. misplacing the records and not organizing the records in proper order within file drawers.
    c. electrical circuit overload, file tipping, and collisions.
    d. carpal tunnel syndrome, electrical circuit overload, and misplacing records within file drawers.

19. _____

**20.** ADA stands for
    a. Americans with Disabilities Act.
    b. American Disabilities Association.
    c. American Database Association.
    d. Association for Directors of America.

20. _____

**21.** Biometric access control devices can evaluate the physical characteristics of a person's
    a. weight.
    b. heartbeat.
    c. eyes.
    d. height.

21. _____

22. Total costs for an automated records management system consist of

    a. overhead, such as costs of heat and electricity.

    b. initial outlay, maintenance, support, and training.

    c. the amount paid for the system software and hardware.

    d. salaries of those operating the system.

22. _____

23. A set of instructions for a computer is a

    a. browser.

    b. hard drive.

    c. pointer.

    d. program.

23. _____

24. A field within a database table whose value is unique within the table and is used to relate a record to one or more records in another table is a

    a. DBMS.

    b. record.

    c. string.

    d. key.

24. _____

25. Paper records should be stored inside a file folder with the front facing the user and the heading to the

    a. right.

    b. left.

    c. top.

    d. bottom.

25. _____

26. The purpose of an authentication system is to

    a. avoid the misplacement of paper records and computer data.

    b. protect the data in a computer or computer network by controlling user access.

    c. protect and control the access to facilities such as office buildings, floors, and rooms.

    d. prevent paper record damage by converting printed text and graphics to computer data.

26. _____

27. The best candidates for subject filing are

    a. numbered forms such as invoices, requisitions, and checks.

    b. employee records such as applications for employment and pay records.

    c. records that refer to products, processes, and formulas.

    d. records that refer to locality, area, or sales territory.

27. _____

28. According to Chapter 12, UPS stands for

    a. United Parcel Service.

    b. uninterruptible power source.

    c. uninterruptible password system.

    d. unidentified password security.

28. _____

**29.** Factors considered in the architecture of an automated records management system include the

    a. quality of the software being purchased.

    b. management functions that the system will perform.

    c. total cost of the automated system.

    d. types of computers on which the software will run.

29. _____

**30.** The person responsible for maintaining the integrity of an organization's records is the

    a. librarian.

    b. administrative assistant.

    c. records clerk.

    d. records and information manager.

30. _____

**31.** The records and information manager exercises records control within the organization by allowing access to records only to

    a. the organization's employees.

    b. authorized persons.

    c. the records clerk.

    d. the administrative assistant.

31. _____

**32.** If a record cannot be found,

    a. it is documented as being lost.

    b. it has no value to the organization.

    c. someone is assigned the job of reconstructing a similar record.

    d. someone is assigned the job of finding the record.

32. _____

**33.** The records and information manager oversees the destruction of records when

    a. the organization is unable to locate or afford additional storage space.

    b. they are no longer needed in the operations of the organization.

    c. they are no longer required for legal reasons.

    d. they are no longer needed in the operations of the organization or required for legal reasons.

33. _____

**34.** The source of information important to the government when determining whether or not a business is abiding by laws and regulations dealing with business is

    a. archival records.

    b. all business records.

    c. active records.

    d. retention records.

34. _____

**35.** The federal law that denies access to one's personal records without his or her permission is the

    a. Federal Reports Act.

    b. Federal Records Act.

    c. Freedom of Information Act.

    d. Privacy Act.

35. _____

**36.** Records and information management professionals often have a    36. _____
   a. master's degree in accounting, finance, or economics
   b. Ph.D. in one of the business disciplines or in information and library science.
   c. two- or four-year degree in business or information and library science.
   d. bachelor's degree in liberal arts, computer science, or environmental engineering.

**37.** An example of copyright infringement is    37. _____
   a. records destruction.
   b. price fixing.
   c. a civil dispute.
   d. software piracy.

**38.** The profession of records and information management consists of    38. _____
   a. two groups: specialists in RIM and those whose occupation includes the management of information but who have another specialty or job title.
   b. two groups: specialists in RIM and computer programmers.
   c. three groups: specialists in RIM, computer programmers, and those whose occupation includes the management of information but who have another specialty or job title.
   d. two groups: those whose occupation includes the management of information but who have another specialty or job title, and computer programmers.

**39.** Admissibility into evidence refers to whether or not    39. _____
   a. a copy of a document will be accepted in court as valid evidence in a lawsuit.
   b. the organization is responsible for gathering, organizing, and presenting its documents as vidence in a lawsuit.
   c. the court is responsible for gathering, organizing, and presenting the organization's documents as evidence in a lawsuit.
   d. the organization is permitted to destroy its documents after they have been presented in a lawsuit.

**40.** ARMA International is a    40. _____
   a. collegiate student organization whose letters stand for Association of Records Managers and Administrators, Inc.
   b. collegiate student organization whose letters stand for Association of Records Managers of America, Inc.
   c. professional association whose letters stand for Association of Records Managers of America, Inc.
   d. professional association whose letters stand for Association of Records Managers and Administrators, Inc.

# True or False
Circle T if the statement is true or F if the statement is false. (1 point each, total 50)

**41.** The three Rs of records and information management are retrieval, retention, and recycling.    41. T F

**42.** Small businesses, manufacturers, and art retailers are examples of the types of organizations likely to employ archivists.    42. T F

**43.** The use of an ergonomic keyboard should be considered as one way to reduce repetitive motion injuries.    43. T F

**44.** It is important for records and information managers to be familiar with criminal and civil laws and regulations.    44. T F

45. The activity of destruction is part of the function of records and information management.   **45.**   T   F

46. A person who is responsible for ensuring the integrity of financial records has the duties of designing records systems, updating records, and designing controls.   **46.**   T   F

47. Cost is one of the five major components in the retrieval function.   **47.**   T   F

48. The federal government allows state governments to determine whether or not citizens have the right to gain access to information about themselves.   **48.**   T   F

49. Plug in and unplug electrical equipment only when the power switch is in the *on* position.   **49.**   T   F

50. Records management deals with paper records, whereas information management deals with computer records.   **50.**   T   F

51. The RIM should consider the costs prior to the selection of a records security system.   **51.**   T   F

52. One may duplicate copyrighted items without permission of the owner if doing so for commercial use.   **52.**   T   F

53. Wills, deeds, birth certificates, marriage records, and tax records are types of legal records that might be kept by a governmental unit such as a city or county.   **53.**   T   F

54. Mail, fax machines, interoffice delivery, and e-mail are methods of distributing records to users.   **54.**   T   F

55. Electronic access to records has become the norm in large organizations in recent years.   **55.**   T   F

56. RIM employees should refrain from destroying records that might be relevant to a lawsuit.   **56.**   T   F

57. Unlike paper records, records stored in electronic databases are free from possible destruction.   **57.**   T   F

58. In the delivery component of retrieval, records are delivered to a records storage area to be filed.   **58.**   T   F

59. Maintaining the integrity of records means that they are kept in fireproof vaults at all times.   **59.**   T   F

60. Employees in medical RIM may have a background in business, medical technology, medical records, nursing, insurance, or health care services.   **60.**   T   F

61. Legal action by the government for noncompliance is a risk the RIM manager must be aware of.   **61.**   T   F

62. A records manager cannot prevent human disasters.   **62.**   T   F

63. The primary purpose of the documentation component of retrieval is to make a record of the location(s) in which documents are filed.   **63.**   T   F

64. In addition to storing and protecting records, depositories and records centers might also film records, destroy records, and recover records after a disaster.   **64.**   T   F

65. Records should be protected from the hazards of fire and floods.   **65.**   T   F

66. Follow-up is the component of retrieval in which records employees communicate with users if borrowed records are due.   **66.**   T   F

67. Equipment and buildings have improved, resulting in disaster preparedness becoming somewhat less important in recent years.   **67.**   T   F

68. The use of professional RIM consultants is decreasing.   **68.**   T   F

69. Developments in technology have made it less tempting to produce paperwork.   **69.**   T   F

70. Both microfilm and microfiche are microrecords.   **70.**   T   F

71. Automated records management systems are software programs that make files, documents, and other records accessible for management by computer.   **71.**   T   F

72. Matters of business ethics have little relevance to the records and information management employee.   **72.**   T   F

73. *Filing* is the key word that should be considered in the storage function of RIM.   **73.**   T   F

74. One of the benefits ARMA members receive from the organization is discounts on filing equipment.   **74.**   T   F

75. A nuclear accident is a human disaster.   **75.**   T   F

76. Good ethical business management by the RIM can result in increased employee loyalty and productivity.   **76.**   T   F

77. CD-R and CD-RW are both ways to convert alphanumeric or graphic information into computer language.      77.   T   F

78. Each incoming piece of paperwork is classified as a record to be kept.      78.   T   F

79. Businesses that establish environmental protection policies do so unnecessarily because the government sets such policies.      79.   T   F

80. Automated records management systems require computer software.      80.   T   F

81. Records retention is probably the most complex and difficult issue that the professional records and information manager must address.      81.   T   F

82. Records are stored and sometimes transferred to an inactive storage area once they are no longer in daily use.      82.   T   F

83. Many records can be saved after being exposed to the heat, smoke, and flames of a serious fire.      83.   T   F

84. Micrographic technology reduces storage space expenses.      84.   T   F

85. Maintaining confidentiality of records is an example of how the records and information manager and employee can observe high ethical standards.      85.   T   F

86. The Institute of Certified Records Managers (ICRM) is the organization that oversees the professional designation of CRM.      86.   T   F

87. Federal, state, and local governments allow organizations to use their own discretion when making decisions about keeping or destroying records.      87.   T   F

88. Mail that comes in on paper is called hard copy mail.      88.   T   F

89. On the Internet, every person who can receive e-mail must have the same address.      89.   T   F

90. A precise retention schedule can be one result of a well-planned retention policy.      90.   T   F

## Alphabetizing

In the blank at the right, indicate the alphabetic order of each name in the series of three names. The first item (0.) is an example. (1 point each, total 10)

  0. (a) Louis Pryor; (b) Lois Pryor; (c) M. Prime      0. cba

91. (a) W. Allen Bernstein; (b) Bernstein-Young Pharmacists; (c) Bryan Bernstein      91. _____

92. (a) Molly's Check Cashing Service; (b) Cora Mollino; (c) Consuelo Moscatt, Jr.      92. _____

93. (a) Tashia & Sam Candies; (b) Tashia Answering Service; (c) The Tashia Flower Shop      93. _____

94. (a) 4th Street Building Co.; (b) 4 Your Wedding Accessories; (c) 40 Mile Beach Hotel      94. _____

95. (a) Public Schools, City of Allentown; (b) Allentown Door Mfg. Co.; (c) Allentown Classroom Supplies      95. _____

96. (a) Braine Co., 226 Moyer Ave., Oakland, CA; (b) Braine Co., Massey Dr., Oxnard, CA; (c) Braine Co., 12472 Moyer Ave., Oakland, CA      96. _____

97. (a) U.S. Dept. of the Interior; (b) United States Gum Co.; (c) United Stay-Fast Inc.      97. _____

98. (a) The Artists House; (b) Artists of Contentment, Inc.; (c) Art by Nicholas, Ltd.      98. _____

99. (a) Albert Beckerman; (b) Bank of the Southwest; (c) Beck's Studios      99. _____

100. (a) The O'Malley's Shop; (b) Sophia O'Malley; (c) Shirley O'Malley      100. _____

# COMPREHENSIVE TEST—FORM B
## Chapters 1–12

## Multiple Choice
In the blank after each item, write the letter of the best response. (1 point each, total 40)

1. ARMA International is a
   a. collegiate student organization whose letters stand for Association of Records Managers and Administrators, Inc.
   b. collegiate student organization whose letters stand for Association of Records Managers of America, Inc.
   c. professional association whose letters stand for Association of Records Managers of America, Inc.
   d. professional association whose letters stand for Association of Records Managers and Administrators, Inc.

   1. _____

2. Admissibility into evidence refers to whether or not
   a. a copy of a document will be accepted in court as valid evidence in a lawsuit.
   b. the organization is responsible for gathering, organizing, and presenting its documents as evidence in a lawsuit.
   c. the court is responsible for gathering, organizing, and presenting the organization's documents as evidence in a lawsuit.
   d. the organization is permitted to destroy its documents after they have been presented in a lawsuit.

   2. _____

3. The profession of records and information management consists of
   a. two groups: specialists in RIM and those whose occupation includes the management of information but who have another specialty or job title.
   b. two groups: specialists in RIM and computer programmers.
   c. three groups: specialists in RIM, computer programmers, and those whose occupation includes the management of information but who have another specialty or job title.
   d. two groups: those whose occupation includes the management of information but who have another specialty or job title, and computer programmers.

   3. _____

4. An example of copyright infringement is
   a. records destruction.
   b. price fixing.
   c. a civil dispute.
   d. software piracy.

   4. _____

**5.** Records and information management professionals often have a

    a. master's degree in accounting, finance, or economics.

    b. Ph.D. in one of the business disciplines or information and library science.

    c. two- or four-year degree in business or information and library science.

    d. bachelor's degree in liberal arts, computer science, or environmental engineering.

**5.** _____

**6.** The federal law that denies access to one's personal records without his or her permission is the

    a. Federal Reports Act.

    b. Federal Records Act.

    c. Freedom of Information Act.

    d. Privacy Act.

**6.** _____

**7.** The source of information important to the government when determining whether or not a business is abiding by laws and regulations dealing with business is

    a. archival records.

    b. all business records.

    c. active records.

    d. retention records.

**7.** _____

**8.** The records and information manager oversees the destruction of records when

    a. the organization is unable to locate or afford additional storage space.

    b. they are no longer needed in the operations of the organization.

    c. they are no longer required for legal reasons.

    d. they are no longer needed in the operations of the organization or required for legal reasons.

**8.** _____

**9.** If a record cannot be found,

    a. it is documented as being lost.

    b. it has no value to the organization.

    c. someone is assigned the job of reconstructing a similar record.

    d. someone is assigned the job of finding the record.

**9.** _____

**10.** The records and information manager exercises records control within the organization by allowing access to records only to

    a. the organization's employees.

    b. authorized persons.

    c. the records clerk.

    d. the administrative assistant.

**10.** _____

**11.** The person responsible for maintaining the integrity of an organization's records is the

    a. librarian.

    b. administrative assistant.

    c. records clerk.

    d. records and information manager.

**11.** _____

12. Factors considered in the architecture of an automated records management system include the

    a. quality of the software being purchased.
    b. management functions that the system will perform.
    c. total cost of the automated system.
    d. types of computers on which the software will run.

12. _____

13. According to Chapter 12, UPS stands for

    a. United Parcel Service.
    b. uninterruptible power source.
    c. uninterruptible password system.
    d. unidentified password security.

13. _____

14. The best candidates for subject filing are

    a. numbered forms such as invoices, requisitions, and checks.
    b. employee records such as applications for employment and pay records.
    c. records that refer to products, processes, and formulas.
    d. records that refer to locality, area, or sales territory.

14. _____

15. The purpose of an authentication system is to

    a. avoid the misplacement of paper records and computer data.
    b. protect the data in a computer or computer network by controlling user access.
    c. protect and control the access to facilities such as office buildings, floors, and rooms.
    d. prevent paper record damage by converting printed text and graphics to computer data.

15. _____

16. Paper records should be stored inside a file folder with the front facing the user and the heading to the

    a. right.
    b. left.
    c. top.
    d. bottom.

16. _____

17. A field within a database table whose value is unique within the table and is used to relate a record to one or more records in another table is a

    a. DBMS.
    b. record.
    c. string.
    d. key.

17. _____

18. A set of instructions for a computer is a

    a. browser.
    b. hard drive.
    c. pointer.
    d. program.

18. _____

19. Total costs for an automated records management system consist of
    a. overhead, such as costs of heat and electricity.
    b. initial outlay, maintenance, support, and training.
    c. the amount paid for the system software and hardware.
    d. salaries of those operating the system.

19. _____

20. Biometric access control devices can evaluate the physical characteristics of a person's
    a. weight.
    b. heartbeat.
    c. eyes.
    d. height.

20. _____

21. ADA stands for
    a. Americans with Disabilities Act.
    b. American Disabilities Association.
    c. American Database Association.
    d. Association for Directors of America.

21. _____

22. Records security measures protect records from different types of risks such as
    a. improper access, accidental loss, theft, damage, and unwanted destruction.
    b. misplacing the records and not organizing the records in proper order within file drawers.
    c. electrical circuit overload, file tipping, and collisions.
    d. carpal tunnel syndrome, electrical circuit overload, and misplacing records within file drawers.

22. _____

23. Information about information is known as
    a. software.
    b. hardware.
    c. metadata.
    d. criteria.

23. _____

24. The purpose of a file guide is to
    a. contain significant correspondence arranged in order by number.
    b. support file folders and to label major sections of the file.
    c. identify the location, area, or territory of the file equipment.
    d. contain significant correspondence arranged in order by date.

24. _____

25. The first step in avoiding injuries in records areas is to
    a. avoid overloading electrical circuits.
    b. avoid tripping over electrical cords on walkways.
    c. speak to the records workers about safety precautions.
    d. develop a written, comprehensive safety plan.

25. _____

26. Major functions of automated records management systems include all of the following except management of
    a. records center employees.
    b. all types of active records.
    c. records for a specific industry.
    d. records retention.

26. _____

27. The procedure of regularly copying the contents of computers onto another medium is called making a(n)

    a. alias.

    b. backup.

    c. attachment.

    d. hyperlink.

27. _____

28. *Larrysmith@majorcorp.com* is a(n)

    a. e-mail address.

    b. Web page.

    c. small computer at Major Corporation.

    d. shortcut to a shared folder.

28. _____

29. An electronic folder that is accessed directly, without the need to access any other folders, is a

    a. directory folder.

    b. root folder.

    c. file folder.

    d. window folder.

29. _____

30. In a file name, July 8 would best be represented in three characters as

    a. J08

    b. JU8

    c. 8JY

    d. 708

30. _____

31. The file name abbreviation that, when pronounced, sounds most like Hannsborough is

    a. Hannsbor.

    b. Hansboro.

    c. Hnnbough.

    d. Hborough.

31. _____

32. The best file name for a letter written on May 4 to Kennitt Company is

    a. Letter

    b. 5_4Letter Kennitt

    c. Kennitt Letter May 4

    d. Kenlet

32. _____

33. To be classified as a record, a piece of paper must be

    a. less costly to the organization when thrown away than when kept.

    b. equal in cost to the organization when thrown away and when kept.

    c. more costly to the organization when thrown away than when kept.

    d. kept temporarily or discarded immediately.

33. _____

34. The following principles should be followed in naming electronic files except

    a. identification.

    b. grammatical correctness.

    c. brevity.

    d. documentation.

34. _____

35. Detailed instructions on a business form should appear

    a. in the right margin.

    b. on the front.

    c. in the left margin.

    d. on the back.

35. _____

36. To save paper when printing reports and other materials,

    a. include headers at the top of each page.

    b. use larger left, right, top, and bottom margins.

    c. single-space and print on both sides of the paper.

    d. use a laser printer.

36. _____

37. The first step in opening the mail in a small organization is to

    a. prioritize.

    b. organize.

    c. classify.

    d. open.

37. _____

38. Creation, distribution, maintenance, protection, control, storage, and destruction describe the

    a. life cycle of records and information management.

    b. duties of the records clerk.

    c. functions of every business and organization.

    d. duties of the administrative assistant.

38. _____

39. A database table is created to hold the names and addresses of all customers. A second table is created to hold all product orders. The two tables are then connected using a

    a. link.

    b. shortcut.

    c. relation.

    d. tether.

39. _____

40. In a database query, the rules that determine what information is displayed are called

    a. query rules.

    b. questions.

    c. criteria.

    d. requests.

40. _____

# True or False

Circle T if the statement is true or F if the statement is false. (1 point each, total 50)

41. A precise retention schedule can be one result of a well-planned retention policy.     41. T F

42. On the Internet, every person who can receive e-mail must have the same address.     42. T F

43. Mail that comes in on paper is called hard copy mail.     43. T F

44. Federal, state, and local governments allow organizations to use their own discretion when making decisions about keeping or destroying records.     44. T F

45. The Institute of Certified Records Managers (ICRM) is the organization that oversees the professional designation of CRM.     45. T F

46. Maintaining confidentiality of records is an example of how the records and information manager and employee can observe high ethical standards.

46. T F

47. Micrographic technology reduces storage space expenses.

47. T F

48. Many records can be saved after being exposed to the heat, smoke, and flames of a serious fire.

48. T F

49. Records are stored and sometimes transferred to an inactive storage area once they are no longer in daily use.

49. T F

50. Records retention is probably the most complex and difficult issue that the professional records and information manager must address.

50. T F

51. Automated records management systems require computer software.

51. T F

52. Businesses that establish environmental protection policies do so unnecessarily because the government sets such policies.

52. T F

53. Each incoming piece of paperwork is classified as a record to be kept.

53. T F

54. CD-R and CD-RW are both ways to convert alphanumeric or graphic information into computer language.

54. T F

55. Good ethical business management by the RIM can result in increased employee loyalty and productivity.

55. T F

56. A nuclear accident is a human disaster.

56. T F

57. One of the benefits ARMA members receive from the organization is discounts on filing equipment.

57. T F

58. *Filing* is the key word that should be considered in the storage function of RIM.

58. T F

59. Matters of business ethics have little relevance to the records and information management employee.

59. T F

60. Automated records management systems are software programs that make files, documents, and other records accessible for management by computer.

60. T F

61. Both microfilm and microfiche are microrecords.

61. T F

62. Developments in technology have made it less tempting to produce paperwork.

62. T F

63. The use of professional RIM consultants is decreasing.

63. T F

64. Equipment and buildings have improved, resulting in disaster preparedness becoming somewhat less important in recent years.

64. T F

65. Follow-up is the component of retrieval in which records employees communicate with users if borrowed records are due.

65. T F

66. Records should be protected from the hazards of fire and floods.

66. T F

67. In addition to storing and protecting records, depositories and records centers might also film records, destroy records, and recover records after a disaster.

67. T F

68. The primary purpose of the documentation component of retrieval is to make a record of the location(s) where documents are filed.

68. T F

69. A records manager cannot prevent human disasters.

69. T F

70. Legal action by the government for noncompliance is a risk the RIM manager must be aware of.

70. T F

71. Employees in medical RIM may have a background in business, medical technology, medical records, nursing, insurance, or health care services.

71. T F

72. Maintaining the integrity of records means that they are kept in fireproof vaults at all times.

72. T F

73. In the delivery component of retrieval, records are delivered to a records storage area to be filed.

73. T F

74. Unlike paper records, records stored in electronic databases are free from possible destruction.

74. T F

75. RIM employees should refrain from destroying records that might be relevant to a lawsuit.

75. T F

76. Electronic access to records has become the norm in large organizations in recent years.

76. T F

77. Mail, fax machines, interoffice delivery, and e-mail are methods of distributing records to users. **77.** T  F

78. Wills, deeds, birth certificates, marriage records, and tax records are types of legal records that might be kept by a governmental unit such as a city or county. **78.** T  F

79. One may duplicate copyrighted items without permission of the owner if doing so for commercial use. **79.** T  F

80. The RIM should consider the costs prior to the selection of a records security system. **80.** T  F

81. Records management deals with paper records, whereas information management deals with computer records. **81.** T  F

82. Plug in and unplug electrical equipment only when the power switch is in the *on* position. **82.** T  F

83. The federal government allows state governments to determine whether or not citizens have the right to gain access to information about themselves. **83.** T  F

84. Cost is one of the five major components in the retrieval function. **84.** T  F

85. A person who is responsible for ensuring the integrity of financial records has the duties of designing records systems, updating records, and designing controls. **85.** T  F

86. The activity of destruction is part of the function of records and information management. **86.** T  F

87. It is important for records and information managers to be familiar with criminal and civil laws and regulations. **87.** T  F

88. The use of an ergonomic keyboard should be considered as one way to reduce repetitive motion injuries. **88.** T  F

89. Small businesses, manufacturers, and art retailers are examples of the types of organizations likely to employ archivists. **89.** T  F

90. The three Rs of records and information management are retrieval, retention, and recycling. **90.** T  F

## Alphabetizing

In the blank at the right, indicate the alphabetic order of each name in the series of three names. The first item (0.) is an example. (1 point each, total 10)

  **0.** (a) Louis Pryor; (b) Lois Pryor; (c) M. Prime      **0.** cba

 **91.** (a) The O'Malley's Shop; (b) Sophia O'Malley; (c) Shirley O'Malley      **91.** _____

 **92.** (a) Albert Beckerman; (b) Bank of the Southwest; (c) Beck's Studios      **92.** _____

 **93.** (a) The Artists House; (b) Artists of Contentment, Inc.; (c) Art by Nicholas, Ltd.      **93.** _____

 **94.** (a) U.S. Dept. of the Interior; (b) United States Gum Co.; (c) United Stay-Fast Inc.      **94.** _____

 **95.** (a) Braine Co., 226 Moyer Ave., Oakland, CA; (b) Braine Co., Massey Dr., Oxnard, CA; (c) Braine Co., 12472 Moyer Ave., Oakland, CA      **95.** _____

 **96.** (a) Public Schools, City of Allentown; (b) Allentown Door Mfg. Co.; (c) Allentown Classroom Supplies      **96.** _____

 **97.** (a) 4th Street Building Co.; (b) 4 Your Wedding Accessories; (c) 40 Mile Beach Hotel      **97.** _____

 **98.** (a) Tashia & Sam Candies; (b) Tashia Answering Service; (c) The Tashia Flower Shop      **98.** _____

 **99.** (a) Molly's Check Cashing Service; (b) Cora Mollino; (c) Consuelo Moscatt, Jr.      **99.** _____

**100.** (a) W. Allen Bernstein; (b) Bernstein-Young Pharmacists; (c) Bryan Bernstein      **100.** _____

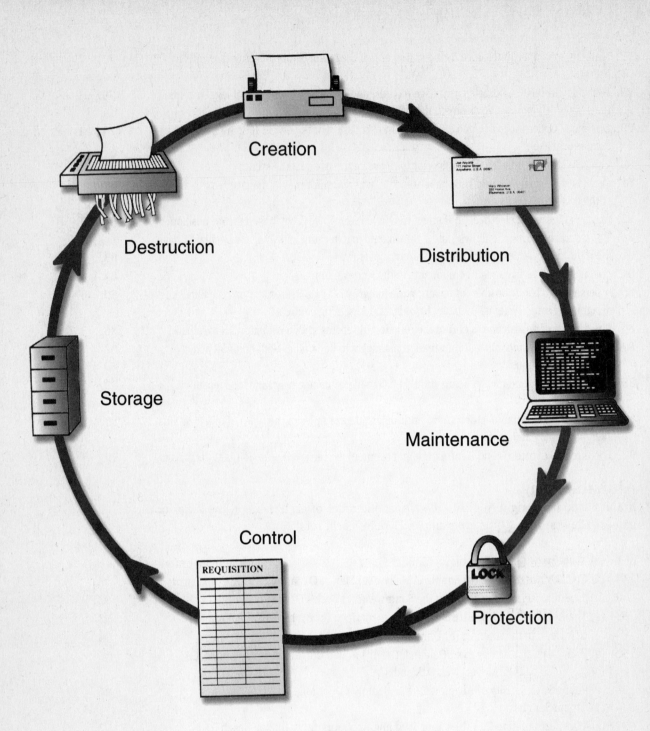

**Figure 1.5**

**The Life Cycle of Records**

Each record goes through this cycle.

# SUGGESTIONS FOR INCORPORATING SCANS COMPETENCIES

Suggested optional activities associated with the Secretary's Commission on Achieving Necessary Skills (SCANS) are listed under each of the five major SCANS competencies.

## Resources—Identifies, organizes, plans, and allocates resources.

*Suggested activity:* On either an individual or small group basis, have students obtain an office supplies catalog that includes prices for filing equipment and supplies. Select a budget amount—perhaps $1,000—and assign students the task of purchasing within the budget a new filing system for a real or hypothetical business. Have students or groups compare their purchasing recommendations. Have them evaluate their purchases on the basis of (1) being within budget, (2) including the necessary equipment and supplies for a new system, and (3) the degree to which the purchases fit the assumed needs of the business.

## Interpersonal—Works with others.

*Suggested activity:* This activity should be performed by groups of three to five students each. Students are to assume that they have purchased a small office supplies store that has two full-time and four part-time employees. The group is to develop a brief employee policy manual for the store that addresses such factors as employee attendance, dress, customer interaction, training, job evaluation, and promotion. Groups may exchange and compare their manuals. Manuals may be evaluated by students and the instructor on the basis of (1) completeness, (2) conciseness, (3) fairness, (4) how reasonable and realistic the policies might be in a real business climate.

## Information—Acquires and uses information.

*Suggested activity:* On either a group or individual basis, have students gather information about the records and information management system of a small business, an office of a larger business, or an office in the school attended by the students. Examples of the information to be acquired are (1) filing systems used, (2) job titles of employees using the system, (3) good and bad features of the systems as perceived by the employees, (4) layout of filing equipment, (5) types of filing supplies used, and (6) projected changes in the filing and records management systems. For this activity, it is suggested that oral reports be given from the notes taken during office visits. Evaluations should be based upon how specific the information is, how comprehensive the coverage is, and how well the information is communicated during the oral presentation.

## Systems—Understands complex interrelationships.

*Suggested activity:* This suggestion is to have students follow up on the Information activity above. Now the student or group develops a new records management system for the office visited. The new system should be justified on the basis of specific information gathered. A written report might include (1) a listing of any new equipment and supplies to be procured, (2) a description of how records are to be filed and disposed of, and (3) an explanation of how technology might be employed to make the system more efficient. The written report may be evaluated by other students or groups and the instructor. The major assessment criterion should be the degree to which the recommendations are likely to bring about greater efficiency and effectiveness in the office and to the business or organization at large.

## Technology—Works with a variety of technologies.

*Suggested activity:* Individuals or groups in this suggested activity assume they are working for a real or hypothetical business. The activity should take place after students have completed all or most of *Professional Records and Information Management*, Second Edition. The task is to determine how the business can better employ technology, including computer technology and the Internet, to manage its information. Students might explore, for example, bar coding of records, filming of documents, e-mail for correspondence, database software, and records management software. It is suggested that reports on this activity be submitted on disk from a word processing program. Evaluation should give attention to (1) the likelihood of suggestions saving time and resources, (2) the degree of sophistication of the technology, and (3) the organization and clarity of the report.

Perhaps you would prefer to create your own SCANS activities. If so, you may want to use the chart below to help you correlate the competencies to the three-part foundations. First, record the chapter number. Next identify the competency and topics under each competency that you want to address. Then asterisk the competencies from the three-part foundations that you would like to include in your activity. Finally, with this information in front of you, write your activity to meet the criteria you have selected.

| CHAPTER | FIVE COMPETENCIES | THREE-PART FOUNDATION | | | | | | | | | | | | | | | |
| | | BASIC SKILLS | | | | | THINKING SKILLS | | | | | | PERSONAL QUALITIES | | | | |
| | | 1. Reading | 2. Writing | 3. Mathematics | 4. Listening | 5. Spelling | 6. Creative Thinking | 7. Decision Making | 8. Listening | 9. Seeing Things in the Mind's Eye | 10. Knowing How to Learn | 11. Reading | 12. Responsibility | 13. Self-Esteem | 14. Sociability | 15. Self-Management | 16. Integrity and Honesty |
| **A. Resources—Identifies, organizes, plans, and allocates resources** | | | | | | | | | | | | | | | | | |
| A1 | Time | | | | | | | | | | | | | | | | |
| A2 | Money | | | | | | | | | | | | | | | | |
| A3 | Material and Facilities | | | | | | | | | | | | | | | | |
| A4 | Human Resources | | | | | | | | | | | | | | | | |
| **B. Interpersonal—Works with others** | | | | | | | | | | | | | | | | | |
| B1 | Participates as a Member of a Team | | | | | | | | | | | | | | | | |
| B2 | Teaches Others New skills | | | | | | | | | | | | | | | | |
| B3 | Serves Clients and Customers | | | | | | | | | | | | | | | | |
| B4 | Exercises Leadership | | | | | | | | | | | | | | | | |
| B5 | Negotiates | | | | | | | | | | | | | | | | |
| B6 | Works with Diversity | | | | | | | | | | | | | | | | |
| **C. Information—Acquires and uses information** | | | | | | | | | | | | | | | | | |
| C1 | Acquires and Evaluates Information | | | | | | | | | | | | | | | | |
| C2 | Organizes and Maintains Information | | | | | | | | | | | | | | | | |
| C3 | Interprets and Communicates Information | | | | | | | | | | | | | | | | |
| C4 | Uses Computers to Process Information | | | | | | | | | | | | | | | | |
| **D. Systems—Understands complex interrelationships** | | | | | | | | | | | | | | | | | |
| D1 | Understands Systems | | | | | | | | | | | | | | | | |
| D2 | Monitors and Corrects Performance | | | | | | | | | | | | | | | | |
| D3 | Improves or Designs Systems | | | | | | | | | | | | | | | | |
| **E. Technology—Works with a variety of technologies** | | | | | | | | | | | | | | | | | |
| E1 | Selects Technology | | | | | | | | | | | | | | | | |
| E2 | Applies Technology to Task | | | | | | | | | | | | | | | | |
| E3 | Maintains and Troubleshoots Equipment | | | | | | | | | | | | | | | | |